THE FENG SHUI KITCHEN

THE FENG SHUI KITCHEN

THE PHILOSOPHER'S GUIDE TO COOKING AND EATING

MASTER LAM KAM CHUEN
WITH LAM KAI SIN

JOURNEY EDITIONS
Boston • Tokyo • Singapore

First published in the United States in 2000 by Journey Editions, an imprint of Periplus Editions (HK) Ltd., with editorial offices at 153 Milk Street, Boston, Massachusetts 02109.

Library of Congress Cataloging-in-Publication Data is on file

ISBN: 1-885203-93-4

Distributed by

USA
Tuttle Publishing
Distribution Center
Airport Industrial Park
364 Innovation Drive
North Clarendon, VT 05759-9436
Tel: (802) 773-8930
Tel: (800) 526-2778

Canada
Raincoast Books
8680 Cambie Street
Vancouver, British Columbia
V6P 6M9
Tel: (604) 323-7100
Fax: (604) 323-2600

Japan
Tuttle Shuppan
RK Building, 2nd Floor
2-13-10 Shimo-Meguro, Meguro-Ku
Tokyo 153 0064
Tel: (03) 5437-0171
Fax: (03) 5437-0755

Southeast Asia (excluding Singapore and Malaysia)
Berkeley Books Pte Ltd
5 Little Road #08-01
Singapore 536983
Tel: (65) 280-1330
Fax: (65) 280-6290

First edition
06 05 04 03 02 01 00   10 9 8 7 6 5 4 3 2 1

Design by Bridget Morley

Printed in Singapore

FENG SHUI

CONTENTS

INTRODUCTION 8

Part Four

THE *Four*

S
E
A
S
O
N
S

110–55

INTRODUCTION

You walk into someone's kitchen and you feel instantly at ease. You walk into someone else's kitchen and you suddenly feel edgy.

You feel a cold coming on and you instinctively know that you want some soup. You are out shopping in summer and find yourself spending more time than usual looking at the range of vegetables.

You go out for a meal with a group of friends. You sit together around the table, feeling nurtured and secure. Next day, back at work, you rush to lunch on your own. Arriving back in the workplace you feel no different: you are still anxious and start thinking about having a snack.

We all have these moments. They are instinctive. They are based on our natural interaction with the world around us. They are not unique to any single culture, even though the ways we behave as a result and the interpretations we place on our behavior vary from culture to culture.

All of us have an intimate and profound relationship with our environment. Our surroundings are constantly affecting us, just as we, at the same time, are leaving our own distinctive imprint on everything around us.

Understanding this relationship is the basis of the ancient Chinese art of Feng Shui (pronounced Fung Shoy). The Chinese characters themselves stand for Wind and Water, two of the elements most essential for human life. Without air, we die within a matter of only a few moments. Without water, we can sustain life only as long as the body's resources last.

These two energies – one invisible, the other visible – can be understood as symbols for the multiple energies of the cosmos. The study of Feng Shui is the study of these energies – their patterns, influences and interactions. In classical Chinese culture, this study was almost entirely confined to the preserve of the Imperial Court. It was a factor in all major decisions affecting the destiny of the empire.

Feng Shui remains an art whose inner essence is transmitted individually from teacher to student. But in recent times its benefits have come to be much more widely shared. This book, and my previous books on Feng Shui, *The Feng Shui Handbook* and *The Personal Feng Shui Manual*, are part of that new openness.

This book aims to help people who want to know how they can arrange their kitchen or cooking area in accordance with basic Feng Shui principles and how to select and prepare meals in harmony with the changing energies of the seasons.

Cooking and eating occupy a central role in Chinese culture. Food is treated as medicine, and cooking is sometimes regarded as one of the healing arts. Food is often at the center of cultural and spiritual pursuits and is a key element in social life as a whole. These aspects often come together, as the photo on the facing page graphically demonstrates. This is an annual event for the whole community, known as the Bun Festival. At its heart are towers of more than 600 buns!

BLEND OF WISDOM

There is a subtle blending of various types of wisdom contained in the classical Chinese approach to food. The story is told of a man walking in the mountains. It is a cloudless summer day. The sun beats down relentlessly. The man comes to a small house near the path and knocks. An old woman comes to the door. He asks her for cool water and stands hesitantly outside. She insists that he come in and sit down. She motions to a place near an inside wall. Although he is obviously in a hurry, she insists on heating the water to make tea. When it is ready, it is too hot to drink and there are rice husks floating on the surface. This angers her visitor: he is forced to sit, waiting for the tea to cool and then pick the floating husks out with his fingers. He leaves without a word of thanks.

Several years later, the same man is walking along the mountain path. He finds the old woman's house and knocks on the door. "I have come to thank you," he says. "It has taken me all this time to realize my good fortune in coming to your door when I wanted water. You could tell I was foolish, walking in the burning sun. You made me come inside, gave me a seat where I would feel protected, and forced me to cool down and rest. That was the reason for the boiling tea with rice husks. I was too stupid to realize your kindness. Please forgive my anger."

This is a story about Feng Shui. The position she chose for her guest was guaranteed to put him at ease, resting with his back against a solid inner wall. It is also a story about Chinese medicine. If she had served him cool water in his overheated condition, it would have caused a powerful and potentially damaging reaction inside his body. The relative cold of the water would have caused his body to retain heat, not release it. Unbeknown to him, the old woman was preventing an attack of heat stroke. The hot tea she gave him was the preventive medicine he needed – the whole process allowed his body to restore itself naturally to its balanced state.

INNER SENSE

Feng Shui corresponds to an inner sense of the world. As you work with the first two parts of this book, you will find much that strikes a chord with your personal experience. For example, there are subtle changes of atmosphere going on all the time. You naturally notice them and they affect your moods. Some rooms make you feel irritable, in others you tend to feel a bit drowsy – other people may put these mood shifts down to your personality, but you know that you are reacting to something very real in the rooms themselves.

If this is true for living rooms and meeting rooms, it is equally true for the kitchen. As this book makes clear, we live in a dynamic universe in which energy is constantly moving, being transformed and influencing whatever other energies it comes in contact with. If food is prepared in a kitchen which is not protected from harmful energies, the food that is stored and prepared there will pick up that negativity. On the other hand, food kept and cooked in a healthy, harmonious kitchen will carry that positive energy with it when it is served and eaten. It is very similar to the everyday fact that we all prefer to eat food cooked in a clean kitchen, rather than a filthy one.

You may look at some aspects of your home and kitchen differently after reading this book. You might find some of the advice irritating. There could be many reasons for this, but a common factor is that there are trends in contemporary kitchen design and decor that run counter to Feng Shui principles. For example, some fashionable designers are fond of using sheet metal, chrome and aluminium extensively in contemporary home kitchens. Feng Shui, on the other hand, seeks a balance between the various elements and materials in the kitchen and a preponderance of any one of them, but especially metal, is not conducive to a harmonious configuration of energies.

In the world of Feng Shui, "matter" and "energy" are not seen as two separate phenomena. As the example of metal in the kitchen shows, all elements are understood as having an energetic power of their own. It is a world view very much in line with the latest developments in atomic science but it is nevertheless one that requires us to look at and live in the world in a way that differs to most conventional perceptions.

A LIVING EXPERIMENT

Feng Shui is a highly evolved system. It is meant to be used intelligently. What this book offers you is a set of basic principles that can be applied in your own home. It is not a rule book. Every person is different, every home is different, every kitchen is different. The best way to approach a book like this is to respect those differences. Perhaps you will find some ideas here that you would like to experiment with. Try them to see if they work in the context of your own home life. If something feels inappropriate or makes you uncomfortable, trust your inner sense.

The first two parts of this book introduce you to the Feng Shui way of looking at things. Part One offers a deeper look at the classical Chinese understanding of energy, the fundamental forces involved in any kitchen from ancient times right through to the present, and the way in which food is viewed from that perspective. Part Two takes you through the basic Feng Shui principles for planning and organizing your kitchen or cooking area.

The next two parts of the book introduce the Chinese art of cooking. Part Three is a survey of ingredients and the distinctive methods in which they are prepared for maximum health value. Part Four is based on one of the most fascinating contributions China has made to world culture – the system of eating in accordance with the seasons. Here you will find a range of recipes specifically chosen because they meet our deep-seated need to live in harmony with earth's profound cycle of change.

Part One

THE *Energy*
OF **F**
O
O
D

THE ENERGY OF FOOD

Feng Shui is the study of energy. The fundamentals of this ancient system rest on a deeper understanding of how energy works in our lives.

As the earliest natural scientists of China studied the world around them, they became fascinated with the forces they could see at work in nature. The very earliest term for what we now call Feng Shui was made up of two characters which meant "looking into the heavens" and "looking at the earth."

You can get a feel for this spirit of natural inquiry in those moments when you are wondering what the day ahead will be like. Perhaps you are wondering what to wear or whether to take an umbrella with you. You look out of the window or step outside the door of your home. You look up into the sky and your eyes survey the world before you. It's as if, in those moments, you were scanning the universe for clues. We want to know what lies ahead and we all do this as if our instincts tell us that the information we need is there and available to us.

Based on exactly that same, but far more prolonged, investigation, the earliest Chinese scholars examined how the information they gleaned could be used to help establish favorable locations for human dwellings and how people's lives could be organized in harmony with the constantly changing patterns of energy in nature.

As their understanding developed, they took a number of factors into account. These included visible realities such as the landscape, the materials used for construction, colors and textures. They also included invisible influences like magnetism, the passage of time and the way everything changes.

Out of this attempt to understand the complex interactions of visible and invisible forces, came one of the most simple, yet profound contributions of Chinese culture to human thought – the understanding of Yin and Yang. This understanding is one of the cornerstones of Feng Shui and, because it is so fundamental, is explained in this first part of the book.

You are also introduced to the Chinese understanding of food. In the Chinese medical model, food is often called "post-natal Chi." The character "Chi" represents the fundamental energy of the universe. It is sometimes called "the breath of heaven." We are born with a plentiful supply of Chi, but it is used up as we grow, live and work. It needs to be restored. The source of that essential replenishment is food. To the Chinese mind, therefore, the vital energy of food is accorded great respect. The energetic properties of different foods – and the ways in which those properties change according to the way food is prepared and cooked – have been carefully studied over the centuries and the resulting wisdom incorporated into the holistic approach of Chinese medicine.

In an era which has become obsessed with speed, it is perhaps inevitable that so many people should suffer from a sadly diminished view of food as a mere facility. Fast food, with little nutritional value, has become an emblem of our times. The very different view presented in this part of the book is the foundation for understanding the rest of the advice given in the later parts.

At the very heart of the energy model described in these pages is a perception of a world which is constantly in motion. Everything is changing from one moment to the next. Nothing remains the same. Even so, we do not inhabit a chaotic universe. We see recurring patterns and the forces of perpetual change seem constantly to be balancing each other. Precisely because of this tendency towards balance, it is possible to live in harmony, rather than in conflict, with the dance of energy we call life.

UNDERLYING FORCES

All this may seem very theoretical and far removed from the practical, down-to-earth business of arranging your kitchen and deciding what meals to cook. But, increasingly, more and more people are beginning to realize that we have gone seriously astray by failing to understand the true nature of what we are actually doing when we prepare and cook food. A kind of mechanical, lifeless approach to food has become widespread which fails to take into account the many essential, but invisible, forces involved. We ignore these at severe cost to our bodily and mental health.

That is why this first part of the book opens with a reminder, on pages 16–21, of the history of cooking and kitchens. While we are tempted to think of modern life as a great advance on that of our early ancestors, it is also important to understand that we are still in contact with the fundamental energies of nature whenever we cook and eat.

It is also important to have a correct understanding of the nature of these pervasive energies. Energy moves. That is its inherent nature. Ordinarily our senses perceive only the most obvious forms of movement, such as the motion of vehicles in the street or tree leaves swaying in the wind. We are far less aware of the subtle ways in which energy circulates soundlessly in our homes or how it vibrates in walls and home decor. Many people have also lost touch with the differing qualities of energy in various foods.

Thus, in this first part of the book, you will find pages 22–9 devoted to the movement of energy. Although we experience much of our life as a progression which seems to be more or less like a straight line from one day and one event to the next, in reality most of our experience is cyclical, like the changes of the seasons. This is central to the understanding of the Chinese approach to food, and forms the basis of the final part of this book which deals with cooking in harmony with the seasons.

ANCIENT RITUAL

Kitchens are among the remains of the very earliest civilizations, some dating back well over 5000 years. These first peoples included the Banpo of northern China. One of their villages has been excavated near the old imperial capital of Xian, now world famous for its vast underground army of terracotta warriors. The treasures found in the Banpo archeological site include food storage jars and cooking implements.

From these and other very early human endeavors, all the culinary traditions of later civilizations have evolved. Many of the most fundamental aspects have remained unchanged over the centuries.

Visit almost any history museum and you are likely to find a life-size model or mural depicting a scene similar to the one you see opposite. It is the prototype of the kitchen in your home. This simple scene is also the ancestor of virtually all other kitchens, from those found in the most elaborate industrial catering operations to the most elegant restaurants.

A cook normally needs the basic elements you see in the picture opposite: Earth, Air, Fire, Water, and Metal. In this primitive setting, the earth is the fundamental platform on which virtually all activities, including cooking, take place. It is also the source of everything that is grown and cooked. The holding properties of the soil are used to make earthenware vessels and utensils.

Food is being prepared at a lakeside. The water will be drunk but it is also essential for preparing and heating food. Later it will be used for cleaning and for putting out the fire.

Once tamed, the principal use of fire from the earliest times was undoubtedly for cooking. Here, the camp fire is fed with wood in the open air.

Despite its vital properties, we often take the air for granted. But little that we see in this scene could take place without it. Without air most living things would perish. It is indispensable to the fire, and the smoke, steam and vaporized oils dissipate into the surrounding atmosphere.

The people pictured here are already familiar with the use of metal. By the time of the Iron Age, people were experimenting with metal and bone hooks to catch fish, using sharpened blades to cut vegetation and meat, and fashioning metal pots for cooking and storage.

EVOLUTIONARY TREND

In some repects decisions about food – where to find it, where to store it, and where to cook it – have determined fundamental questions about where to live. This has been true not only for individual families, but entire villages and civilizations. Famine and drought have been two of the most powerful causes behind large-scale movements of populations throughout history.

The development of agriculture is widely recognized as having changed numerous aspects of the lives and social structures of peoples for whom hunting was their sole method of procuring food.

Whether the decisions were about where to live or how to establish reliable systems for food procurement and preparation, people in widely differing lands and cultures faced common questions. Is there an easily accessible food source? Is there a reliable source of water nearby? Are there sufficient fuel resources for cooking? Will it be possible to store reasonable quantities of food during the different seasons?

Cooking raises other questions as well. Food attracts predators, both animal and human. How can it be stored safely and securely? Fire and water are both dangerous elements. How can homes be protected from possible water damage and the risk of fire?

Throughout history, different communities have developed their own distinctive answers to these questions. Some took the risk of living and cooking in the same space, often because they had no realistic alternative. Others lived in separate family dwellings, but cooked collectively either in purpose-built structures or the open air.

As Chinese culture developed, great emphasis was placed on separating spaces according to their specific functions. This led to the construction of housing which, as far as possible, clearly distinguished between the areas set aside for various human functions.

The picture on the facing page shows a well-to-do 19th-century Ching dynasty mansion where the main home is reserved for receiving guests, studying, dining and sleeping, but where other activities, including food preparation, take place in smaller separate buildings.

To the rear of this classical Chinese house, at the far end of the courtyard, was a series of small buildings. One was the bathhouse. One was the laundry. The third was the kitchen. All three were near a water supply, normally a well. By housing the kitchen away from the main dwelling, the family was protected from the fire, smoke, cooking odors, and the general commotion of food preparation. Food was transported from the kitchen to the main house (and dishes removed) along a covered walkway.

TODAY'S HEARTH

A contemporary kitchen (see opposite) seems a far cry from the open fire of our earliest ancestors or the wood fires and pantries of a bygone age. But from the Feng Shui point of view it consists of the same five fundamental elements: Earth, Air, Fire, Water, and Metal.

Our ancestors lived and cooked literally on the earth. Nowadays we have constructed so many ways of trying to protect ourselves from calamity that we are in danger of forgetting the earth. It is always beneath us, supporting us. Everything we cook and eat comes from it. It is the source of all nurture and nourishment.

Our forebears' open fires have evolved into modern ovens and stovetops. Instead of wood, we rely on electricity, gas, and other sources of energy. But no matter what fuel we use, this Fire energy is still our hearth. It is the heart of the kitchen and, in many respects, the heart of our home.

We cannot cook in an airless room. Good ventilation is essential, just as it was when our ancestors relied on the open air around them. We not only need air coming in, we also need to ensure that noxious fumes and cooking odors are expelled. Unlike our ancestors, who could rely on the atmosphere around them to absorb smoke and smells, we now have to take care that our indoor kitchens don't pollute our homes.

We need water when we cook. It is indispensable. The nearby river, lake, or village well has now been transformed into the domestic supply of running water. But like all Water energy, it needs to be treated with respect and great care.

It is almost inconceivable to find a kitchen anywhere in the world today without finding something metal in it. Even the humblest cook needs a pot and a knife.

THE ENERGY CYCLE

The kitchen is a place of transformation, a place where many energies intersect. Everything that is brought into the kitchen is changed in some way. This process of change is part of a far larger cycle of energy – a cycle that includes not only the preparation and cooking of food, but the entire process of life itself.

During the T'ang Dynasty (618–906 CE) the Taoist master, Lü Yen, often known as Ancestor Lü, wrote of the energy which pervades the entire universe: "In heaven, energy is substance and form, yin and yang, the motion of the sun, moon, and stars, the waxing and waning of the moon. It is clouds, mist, fog, and moisture. It is the heart of all living beings, their ripening and their growth.

"On earth, energy is power, fuel, the essence of everything that lives, the source of mountain streams. It is the ebb and flow of life, it sets everything in motion and holds all that exists. It is the movement of time, maturing and aging, rising and falling. In humans, it is the life force, movement, action, speech, and perception. It is the spirit of life moving in the body, the gateway to living and dying."

This understanding of life as a vast cycle of energy is beautifully expressed in the art of Chinese landscape painting. In the detail reproduced opposite, the painter evokes the swirling movement of energy in the natural world. Yet, at the same time, all the elements in the panorama are balanced.

The soft, yielding leaves (Yin) are balanced by the solidity of the rocks (Yang). The dynamic force of the water (Yang) is balanced by the quiescence of the mountains (Yin). The cool groves (Yin) are balanced by the heat of the daytime (Yang). The light falling on the high peaks (Yang) is balanced by the shadows in the lower valley (Yin).

The artist, however, is presenting us with more than a set of opposites. An entire cycle of transformation is depicted – symbolizing the process of unending change in the natural world. In this painting, as in numerous classical landscapes, the medium of change is the water element.

As the waters tumble over the rocks and spread out into the valleys, the heat of the sun transforms their passage into mist which rises upward, obscuring the mountains from view. It is a cycle also enacted as water is taken in and released by each leaf and plant on the slopes. The cycle permeates the four seasons, with droplets taking new forms as hailstones, snowflakes, and ice crystals.

In order to understand the world of Feng Shui and the art of Chinese cooking, it is important to understand the poetic logic of this landscape. You are looking at a particular illustration of water, rocks, and trees, but in the mind of the artist, and in the mind of the trained observer, it is also a portrait of the universe. The brush strokes depict all the fundamental elements of life and the profound processes of change without which those elements would be lifeless.

As you will see later in this book, the same logic applies to the arrangement of your kitchen and the preparation of even the simplest meal. It is possible to approach both so that you are able to live, cook, and eat in accordance with the dynamic harmony of nature.

The energy cycle of cascading water
and rising mist is evoked in the
simple brushstrokes of a master artist.

SUN AND RAIN

Within the natural cycle of life on earth, there are polarities of such influence that we tend to think of them as completely different states. Most of us think of day and night in this way and we often plan what we will do, who we will see, what we will wear, and what we will eat according to the daylight hours and night time.

The interplay of sun and rain has a similarly profound effect on our beings, although, unlike the regularity of day and night, the shift from one to the other is often more unpredictable. Nevertheless, whether we normally experience a prolonged period of sunshine followed by a rainy season or whether sun and rain come and go intermittently, both have a distinct effect on our bodies and minds.

The sun's energy opens us up. We feel uplifted. We have more energy and we feel more alive. This is true whether we are out in the sunlight, whether we are just going about our life indoors on a summery day or whether we are spending time in a reasonably warm, dry environment where we feel comfortable and energized. Our internal organs tend to relax and expand when they are warm. Our blood flows more quickly. Our digestive processes work faster.

Heat has the same effect on our mental and emotional powers. We tend to open up, we are more expansive. We communicate more freely. We are more passionate. Life seems more intense to us.

As we warm up internally, however, there is a risk that we might overheat and start to dry out. Our bodies naturally start to adjust to this. We become aware of feeling thirsty and we start to consume liquids. We feel the need to calm down and we take a short break. Our appetite is affected, as are the foods we naturally want to eat; our summer diet is very different to our diet in winter.

When it is overcast and dark or when we are cold, our natural reaction is to close down. We withdraw our energy inward. We instinctively protect ourselves from inclement weather. We start to use up our energy reserves to keep ourselves warm. Our circulation slows down and our digestion becomes more sluggish.

The shadows, cold, and damp depress us. We are less alert. We become more introverted. We talk less. We become more obsessed with ourselves and less interested in others. Our internal energy feels blocked, like a river heavy with silt.

If the damp and cold persist, there is a risk that our inner environment will be seriously affected. Our vital organs, our blood, and our flesh will suffer. If we have chronic poor circulation, conditions such as arthritis may develop. Our natural reaction is to find ways to warm ourselves up and to expel the damp from our bodies. On cold, wet days we develop an appetite for hot foods and warming broths. If we feel sluggish, we might go to the gym where we feel better for sweating out the dampness that has started to make its way into our bodies.

These natural processes of balancing heat and cold, dampness and dryness, have been studied by Chinese natural scientists and physicians over the centuries. Their insights form the basis of much Chinese medical practice, but have also had a profound influence on the entire approach to cooking and eating. The underlying aim is to understand the fundamental processes of nature and to live and eat in ways that keep us in harmony with the changing world around us.

YIN AND YANG

One of the most fundamental ideas running through the whole of Chinese culture is the theory of Yin and Yang. You find it at the heart of almost all the great contributions that China has made to world civilization, from early natural sciences to the development of herbal medicine, from acupuncture to the design of ornamental gardens and the techniques of brush painting. The Yin and Yang philosophy is also the basis of Chinese cuisine, from the most elaborate state banquet to the simplest of meals at home.

The easiest way to understand Yin and Yang is to look out of the window. In the early morning, when the sun's rays first appear, you can see them starting to glance across the leaves on the trees, or the stonework on the wall. There is a natural feeling of warmth, of movement, even of expectation. That which was dark is becoming light. This sense of energy is called Yang. The Chinese character for Yang shows a hillside bathed in the light of the sun once it has risen above the horizon. The brush strokes imitate rays of light streaming down towards the earth.

Look out the window later in the day. The same leaves are in shadow, the sunlight no longer splashing on the stonework. That which was light is heading towards the dark. What was Yang is now Yin. The Chinese character for Yin shows a hillside when the shadows of clouds have fallen over it. This is combined with a few strokes that show people gathered together under one roof.

China's earliest natural scientists were absorbed in the meticulous contemplation of these very simple phenomena. Looking out of your

window in the morning and afternoon are the first steps in understanding Yin and Yang. To really penetrate this mystery you need to take a little more time. Pick a comfortable chair and just sit by the window. Or you can go into your garden or to a park. Any time of day will do, but early to mid-morning on a fairly clear day is probably best – then it is easiest to chart the course of sun and shadow.

When you have picked your spot, look around for something that catches your attention. It might be a nearby house or a group of bushes. Ideally, look for something that is partly in the light and partly in shadow. For example, a house with a sloping roof will naturally have shadows under the eaves. When you have selected your object of contemplation, watch what happens.

Slowly but surely the light moves. The shadows move. The quality of the light

changes. The tones of the shadows change. There is energy in both the light and the dark, but there is a difference between the two. Both have their own power, just as night and day have their distinctive force. At the same time, however, while they are distinguishable from each other, they are also inseparable. Day cannot exist without night, nor the night without the day.

As you watch the play of light and shadow, you see them slowly changing into each other. What was Yang becomes Yin. What is now Yin will become Yang.

NATURAL   BALANCE

The energies of Yin and Yang are constantly seeking to balance each other. But they are never static, any more than is life itself. The interplay between the two is forever in motion, forever dynamic.

"Yin and Yang alternate perpetually between movement and stillness, working and resting," says the Chinese classic, *The Book of Balance and Harmony*. "All things have their origin, development, fulfillment, and procreation. This is the process of the four seasons and the cycle of the year. Each change is a transformation."

Everything in our lives can be understood in terms of this constant interplay of Yin and Yang. That which is uppermost is Yang. Therefore the sky, the human head, and the top of anything is Yang. That which is lowermost is Yin. Therefore the earth, our feet, and the bottom of anything is Yin. That which is strong and bright – the sun, candlelight, fire – is Yang. That which is soft and deep – the night sky, darkness, water – is Yin. Neither Yin nor Yang can exist without the other, any more than light can exist without darkness or a top can exist without a bottom.

These qualities of Yin and Yang are not rigidly fixed. They express a relationship, reflecting the interaction and interpenetration of everything that exists. Thus the sun is Yang in relation to the moon, whose reflected light is Yin. But the light of the moon when seen against the night sky is Yang. Similarly, the sky is Yang in relation to the earth which is below it.

But the spinning and rotating earth is Yang in relation to the stillness of space.

The relationship between Yin and Yang is dynamic. Yin is constantly changing into Yang and Yang is perpetually being transformed into Yin. When you get up in the morning, the Yin state of sleep is transformed into the Yang state of wakefulness.

As the day unfolds you become active. Your body warms up, you express yourself and you exude energy. This is the full power of Yang. But just before you peak, you start to feel a need for refreshment. The nurturing power of Yin has been born out of the fullness of Yang. You have a snack. You feel replenished and you return to work. The regeneration of Yin has in turn given birth again to Yang.

At each point in this constant flux and interchange, Yin and Yang are in balance. It is a subtle process, just as slight movements of the counterweight in the scales pictured here balance the mass in the weighing pan.

The harmony of Yin and Yang is fundamental to the art of Chinese cooking. Even the simplest of meals is based on a balance between Yin and Yang in the foods themselves, and restoring internal harmony in the people who eat them.

This idea was expressed by the great Taoist master, Lao Tse: "Ensure there is balance and harmony, and that heaven and earth are in place, then countless beings will grow."

The Chinese symbol for Yin and Yang is a single circle divided by a symmetrical curve. One half is light, the other is dark. The light portion represents Yang energy, the dark portion symbolizes Yin energy. Each portion is shaped like a tear drop, thin at one end, full at the other. They fit perfectly together so that where Yang is fullest, Yin is just beginning. If you follow the curve around, Yin has reached its maximum and Yang has diminished accordingly. At any point on the curve, both are in balance. Inside each of the two halves, there is a small circle, like a round seed, showing that Yang gives birth to Yin and Yin gives birth to Yang.

FOOD AS MEDICINE

The common expression, "you are what you eat," conveys a truth that has been part of Chinese culture for centuries. You can also change what you are and how you feel by what you eat. We do this every day without particularly thinking about it. If it is cold outside, we love a bowl of hot soup. If it is raining, there is a slump in ice cream sales. If we are sad, we might feel like having something sweet, or perhaps we just don't eat anything at all.

In most traditional cultures, and still today, the moment we start to get a cold, our mothers or grandmothers will start to prepare the family's special broth. They don't tell us they are giving us medicine, but that's what's really going on.

One of the earliest known references to the concept of food as medicine dates back to the oldest and most influential book in the history of world medicine, The Yellow Emperor's *Classic of Internal Medicine* (Huang Ti Nei Ching). It is thought to have been written about 4000 years ago. It is written in the form of a dialogue between the Emperor Huang Ti and the imperial physician, Ch'i Po.

The emperor asks his physician about the origins of disease: "Everything appears to be subject to the pervasive influence of the four seasons and the interaction of Yin and Yang. Is it possible to understand the extent of these influences?"

"Excellent question!" answers the court physician. He describes in detail the five natural influences of dryness, wind, cold, heat, and humidity. Each, he says, has a specific effect on the internal organs and each is related to a particular flavor. Thus, dryness affects the lungs and is related to pungent flavors. Wind affects the liver and is related to sour flavors. Cold affects the kidneys and is related to salty flavors. Heat affects the heart and is related to bitter flavors. Humidity affects the stomach and is related to sweet flavors.

The physician Ch'i Po explains to the emperor: "If there is an excess of salt in the food, the pulse stiffens, the eyes water and the complexion is affected. If the food is too bitter, the skin ages, and body hair is lost. If the food is too pungent, the muscles become knotted, and the finger and toenails start to decay. If the

food is too sour, the flesh hardens,
wrinkles appear, and the lips become weak.
If the food is too sweet, the bones start to
ache and the head hair falls out. These are
the conditions that can result from these
five flavors."

Ch'i Po then explains how the various
flavors interact and can be used to
counteract the various effects of each other.
For example, he tells the emperor: "Sour
flavors are not good for the muscles, but
pungent flavors will counteract this." He
says that bitter flavors will strengthen the
heart, which in turn will nourish the blood
and enliven the stomach.

Out of this careful observation of the
natural influences upon the workings of the
human body has grown the Chinese art of
choosing and preparing food so that each
meal can be seen as a therapeutic treatment,
balancing the constantly changing
influences of the seasons, the weather, and
even our emotional states.

*The woodcut (left) is one of the few existing portraits
of Huang Ti, the Yellow Emperor, whose* Classic of
Internal Medicine *(above) is the foundation of
traditional Chinese medicine. Not only is Chinese
medicine the oldest continuous scientific tradition in
the world, it has also developed the most extensive
pharmacopoeia, with a much greater range of natural
products than any other known medical system.*

MEDICINAL FOODS

The abundant fertility of the earth offers us an extraordinary range of foodstuffs, many of which we use as daily medicine. Others we reserve for times when we feel the need of the unique properties of certain foods. This understanding of food is not unique to Chinese culture. More than 2000 years ago, Hippocrates, one of the founders of the Western medical tradition, wrote: "Each of the substances in people's diets acts upon their bodies and changes them in some way. People's lives depend upon these changes, whether the individuals are in good health, ill, or convalescing."

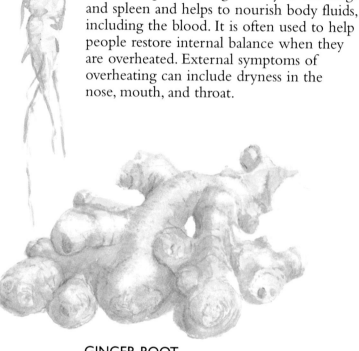

AMERICAN GINSENG

The effect of ginseng is to calm the body and restore harmony to the internal organs. Its properties are fundamentally Yin. This restorative power brings vitality to the lungs and spleen and helps to nourish body fluids, including the blood. It is often used to help people restore internal balance when they are overheated. External symptoms of overheating can include dryness in the nose, mouth, and throat.

GINGER ROOT

In Chinese herbal medicine, ginger is valued for its Yang qualities. Old dry ginger root is particularly prized and is said to combine the properties of ginseng, onion, and garlic. Ginger is a great aid to digestion and is recommended for the prevention of nausea and the relief of indigestion. It stimulates the circulation, and dislodges phlegm and mucus. A recent European medical study has confirmed the traditional use of ginger for rheumatism and arthritis without harmful side effects, reducing swelling and stiffness in the joints.

ONION

The remarkable properties of onions give them both Yin and Yang powers. Onions can help to increase internal energy. They have a particularly positive effect on the lungs, relieving congestion in airways and easing bronchial constriction. They have a natural antibiotic action and are often recommended as a way of reducing the risk of heart disease and stroke.

GARLIC

Belonging to the same family as onions, garlic is a Yang food. Its strong antibiotic action is widely used to fight infection. It helps to keep the heart healthy, promotes circulation, and lowers high blood pressure. It is used by people with diabetes because it lowers blood sugar levels. Chinese population studies have shown that people who usually eat lots of garlic have less than half the risk of stomach cancer than those who eat hardly any.

CARROT

The orange pigment in carrots has anti-oxidant properties. Studies have shown that people who eat foods rich in this pigment have a lower risk of heart disease, stroke, cataracts, and some forms of cancer. A nourishing Yin food, carrots are also thought to counteract the effect of other substances that can cause food poisoning.

SPINACH

High in vitamin A, vitamin C, and potassium, it is not by accident that Popeye called for his spinach when he needed to boost his Yang power. The potassium helps to prevent and regulate high blood pressure. Studies on skin, lung, stomach, bladder, and prostate cancers indicate that people who eat plenty of green leafy vegetables, such as spinach, are less likely to develop tumors; they are also likely to be less at risk from heart disease and stroke.

Part Two

Feng Shui

ESSENTIALS

FENG SHUI ESSENTIALS

Your kitchen is a place of power. In most homes, the kitchen contains more forms of energy than any other room. No matter how basic or high-tech your kitchen is, you rely on all the five fundamental forms of energy for preparing and cooking. You need earth, metal, water, wood, and fire in at least one of their manifestations. The presence of all these energies in one location is a distinctive feature of virtually every kitchen.

Not only is the full spectrum of energy displayed in your kitchen, the intensity of energy is usually far greater than that found anywhere else in your home. For example, the most explosive energy in the home is usually found in electrical equipment and other devices that generate heat. In most contemporary homes, even with the profusion of all types of electronic gadgetry, the kitchen is still likely to contain the greatest number of appliances that consistently require the highest levels of electrical power or that generate the most extreme temperatures.

Even if you turn on all the lights in your living room or study, turn up the volume on your music system, switch on your television and your computer and run a hot bath all at the same time, you are unlikely to reach the energy levels that are generated by normal use of the technology in your kitchen.

Other forms of energy – wood, water, metal, and earth – are also present in abundance in your kitchen. Conventionally, we tend to think of these as matter rather than energy. For example, we think that the tea kettle is made of solid metal. We regard the water that we fill it with as a liquid form of matter. It is only when we turn on the stove to boil the water that we think of energy being involved.

But the first lesson of Feng Shui is that our entire world is energy. What appears to be solid metal or fluid water is just as much a configuration of energy as the electrical power that causes the kettle to heat and water to boil. The different patterns of energy have distinctive behaviors and interact in a variety of ways. For example, we know that the molecular structure of metal is relatively dense. This makes it particularly strong and capable of penetrating other less dense molecular patterns, such as wood. But highly agitated energy, such as heat, increases the rate at which the metal molecules vibrate. The result is that the metal becomes warmer, expands and becomes more pliant. Eventually, it will be transformed into liquid.

None of this is new or surprising to a scientist. What is startling is that this view of the world as the dance of energy was developed so many centuries ago in ancient China through the patient and minute observation of nature. It formed the basis of the art of Feng Shui and can still be applied in the 21st century.

Through their study of energy, the early Feng Shui masters perceived that the different patterns of energy in our environment could also have a profound influence on our own individual energy fields, affecting both our bodies and minds. For example, our bodies react differently to the seasonal changes of summer and winter. Our thoughts and feelings are similarly affected by variations in color, sound, and smell. Different energy patterns can also conflict with each other, disturbing our nervous system and affecting our concentration.

If meals are prepared in an environment of disturbed or even conflicting energy, that turmoil is easily absorbed into the food and then transmitted to all who eat it. Far from being a source of positive nourishment, the food becomes a bridge or conduit for the transfer of negative energy.

This principle was understood by the classical Feng Shui masters who attempted to plan human habitats so that they would provide safe havens in harmony with the diverse energies of the world around them. Thus, arranging your kitchen in accordance with Feng Shui principles is a way of ensuring that the energetic field is as balanced as possible. This is not at all the same as having it planned by an interior designer.

For example, in some countries it has been fashionable to have entirely metallic work surfaces and wall coverings in the kitchen. From the Feng Shui point of view, a domestic kitchen furnished in this way has an overwhelming preponderance of metal energy which is out of balance with the scale of other energies. This is not the case in large commercial kitchens where the overall scale of the other energy patterns is very different to a normal home. This imbalance in an ordinary kitchen creates a subtle unease and harshness which affects not only the nervous system of the cook, but also the meals prepared in that atmosphere.

To ensure a harmonious blend of energy in a kitchen, it is important not only to have a balance of forces within the cooking area itself, but also to ensure that it is well placed and protected within the home. A Feng Shui master takes the total energy field as the starting point – first the location of your home and then the location of your kitchen within it. Seen from this viewpoint, your home is like a flowing river: your kitchen is a strong vortex of energy affected by, but also exerting a strong influence on, the river current. Learning to see your home and kitchen in this way is explained on pages 38–41.

The distinctive patterns of energy can be identified and their qualities understood, as well as their effects on human beings. This wisdom is based on common sense and the observation of everyday life. Flames shoot upwards, they warm and excite us. Water seeks the lowest level. It tends to cool and calm us. Two systems for analysing the energies in your kitchen, known in Feng Shui as the Five Animals and the Five Energies, are presented on pages 42–51.

These ways of understanding the energies in your kitchen can then be applied to virtually all the aspects of this distinctive area of your home, as explained in detail on pages 52–69.

The best Feng Shui advice is to prepare and cook food in a room that is separated from the rest of your living space. Of course, we cannot all afford that luxury but Feng Shui principles can still be applied to single rooms or open-plan apartments in order to create the best possible environment (see pp. 70–1).

THE ENERGY FIELD

Your home is a field of energy. If you were to place it under a huge magnifying glass, you would see it in its entirety in stunning clarity. If you were to increase the magnification up to the power of an ordinary microscope, nothing would seem solid: you would start to see the minute particles of which solid matter seems to be composed.

If you were able to place your home under the world's most powerful electron microscope, it would seem to have dissolved. You would be able to glimpse the traces left by subatomic impulses. Seen as a whole your home would resemble a matrix of fluctuating signals forming a standing wave pattern in space.

The early natural scientists of China established the first principles of Feng Shui from this perception of the world as a web of interpenetrating energies.

The primary principle is that energy moves. Ordinarily our senses perceive the most obvious forms of motion – traffic passing by in the street or the cool rush of the wind against the skin. We are less conscious of the subtle movements of energy as it passes invisibly through the space of an open room or the vibration of the patterns of energy in the walls and furnishings.

Subtle movements of energy are unfolding all the time, like invisible designs weaving their way through space. In most circumstances, the natural tendency of energy is to circulate in a series of curves, sometimes sweeping around a room in a single wave, sometimes more forcefully spinning through the space.

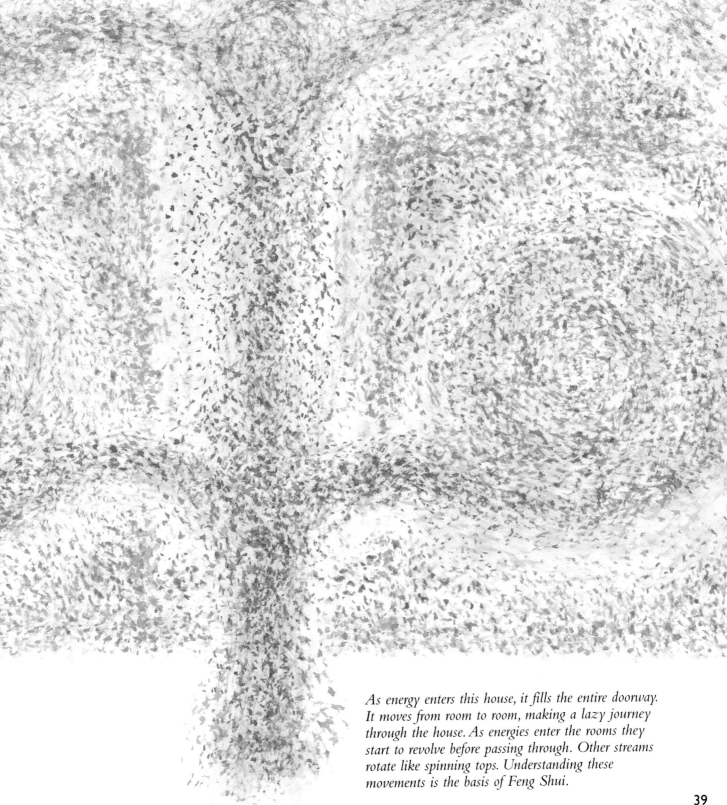

As energy enters this house, it fills the entire doorway. It moves from room to room, making a lazy journey through the house. As energies enter the rooms they start to revolve before passing through. Other streams rotate like spinning tops. Understanding these movements is the basis of Feng Shui.

KITCHEN POSITIONS

Within the field of energy in your home the location of the kitchen is of considerable importance. Wherever possible, your kitchen should be protected from incoming energy that may be harmful, such as that entering through the front door (see facing page). The heat of cooking and the vapors it releases into the air should not be permitted to pollute the rest of your house. For this reason it is better to have a kitchen that doesn't open on to your living room or bedroom. If it does, keep your kitchen door closed, preferably at all times, but especially when preparing food and cooking.

In the energy field shown in the house below, there is a direct line of movement between the kitchen and the bathroom/toilet. This two-way stream leads to a mingling of energies between the two rooms. This is not recommended in Feng Shui. The functions of these two rooms are completely opposite and the distinctive qualities of their energies are not compatible. Every effort should be made to separate these rooms. The negative effect of their juxtaposition in the house shown below would be greatly reduced if the doors to both rooms were kept closed.

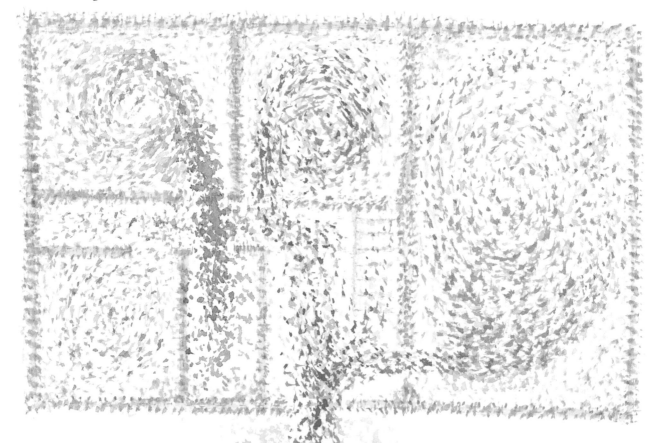

The invading energy that enters the house shown above does not penetrate the kitchen, in the upper left of the plan, because the kitchen door is closed. The closed door also stops fumes and vaporized cooking oils condensing on walls and surfaces throughout the rest of the house.

The kitchen at the top end of this house (right) is completely unprotected from harmful impulses that penetrate the home when the front door is open. The incoming energy slices through the kitchen. This structural defect can be remedied by installing a door or screen partway between the kitchen and the front door, or by keeping your back door closed, especially when the front door is open.

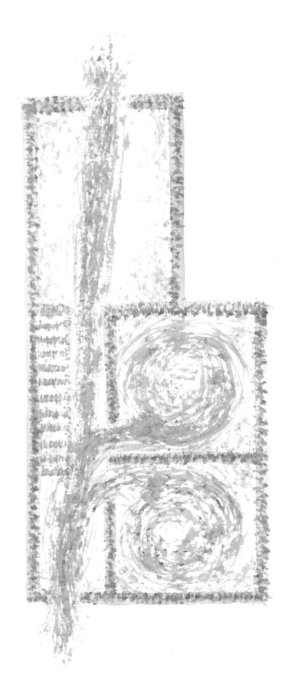

THE KITCHEN LANDSCAPE

Your kitchen is a landscape. The way you arrange that landscape and place yourself in it determines the energy that affects you as you cook. To help you plan the landscape of your kitchen, you can use a ground plan whose basic principles are described in Feng Shui using the symbols of The Five Animals.

The basic elements of the landscape are shown on the opposite page. Imagine you are standing in the centre of the yellow square with your back to the large round hill. The high peaks are to your left. To your right are the low wooded slopes. In front is open space reaching into the distance.

The five symbolic animals that correspond to this physical landscape are shown in the inset on this page. The central space of the landscape is symbolized by a wise serpent, facing forward. The peaks rising to the left are represented by a dragon. To the right, among the low hills, is the region of the tiger. The mountain at the rear is thought of as the tortoise. The open space in front is symbolized by the mythic flying phoenix.

In classical China, these animals were understood to correspond to the various seasons and elements – and were assigned specific colors. The tortoise corresponds to the season Winter and represents the element Water. Its traditional color is blue or black. The dragon's season is Spring, and its element Wood. Its predominant color is green. The phoenix is Summer and Fire. Its symbolic color is red. The tiger evokes Autumn and Metal. Its corresponding colors are white and gold. The central serpent represents the central pivot of the seasons and the earth itself and is depicted in the yellow-brown tones of the soil.

There is an inner logic to these five symbolic animals. The tortoise, with its strong shell, is stable and secure. It protects the central space from any form of disturbance from behind.

The dragon rests high in the clouds. It rises to the left, effortlessly absorbing information from the world spread before it.

The phoenix flies far ahead to the front, representing our capacity for vision, excitement, and inspiration.

The tiger evokes physical strength and violence. Its immense energy is both useful and dangerous. Its power is always ready to be unleashed and needs to be carefully controlled. Its low position on the right of the landscape symbolizes this quality of powerful energy being kept under control.

Coiled at the center, the serpent is protected by the four outlying creatures. It is the general in command of all the forces – protected, well informed, prescient, powerful, and ready for action.

THE KITCHEN ANIMALS

You can use the landscape of the Five Animals to arrange your kitchen so that it is a harmonious environment in which to prepare and cook your meals.

Draw the floor plan of your kitchen or stand in it so that you are facing the stove. In this position, you are the serpent at the center of the landscape. Taking this direction as your fundamental point of reference, you can begin to plan your kitchen. You can arrange the layout of the facilities and equipment in accordance with the positions of the symbolic animals that should be surrounding you in their respective locations. You can check to see if your current kitchen layout matches the correct alignment of the animals.

Behind you is the position of the tortoise. This is where you want security and freedom from fear. When your attention is fully engaged with cooking, you want to be free from any subconscious worries about being disturbed or attacked from the rear.

To your right is the tiger. This is the region of rolling hills, where intense and unpredictable energy needs to be kept under control, like a tamed wildcat.

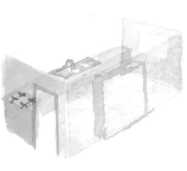

It is important to use common sense. In this very narrow kitchen, the stove has been put right next to the doorway – in an effort to place it against the phoenix wall. But unfortunately the result is that anyone coming into the kitchen risks bumping against the cook.

In this case safety comes first. It is better to place the stove in a location where the cook and everyone else will be less likely to have accidents. Here, the stove is positioned against the tiger wall. The storage cupboards in both are properly placed on the dragon wall.

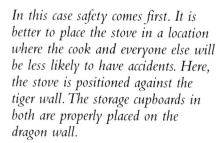

To your left is the dragon. This is the location for high storage cupboards or tall, upright facilities such as large refrigerators and freezers. Their relatively calm energies rise slightly above us, like dragons lazily resting in the clouds.

You are the serpent — wise, creative, and intelligent. You are facing forward toward the stove, which is the modern-day equivalent of the family hearth. The wall behind the stove corresponds to the phoenix, the red-hued bird of perpetual inspiration. If possible, that should be the wall in which there is the principal doorway in and out of the kitchen.

45

KITCHEN DESIGN

A fundamental principle of Feng Shui is that there should be a clear distinction between different functions within the home. At first glance it is hard to tell exactly what you are looking at in the central picture here. Part of it looks like a living room with a soft sofa and fireplace, part of it serves as a dining area and the rest is clearly a kitchen. Whatever you do in this multipurpose room, you are likely to be disturbed. Even the cooking odors and the smoke from the open fireplace will get mixed up together.

The two smaller photographs show designs that do not suffer from this confusion. If the kitchen area is well defined, you can have a small table in it for informal meals. In the upper left photo, the table has a space of its own within the kitchen. The extractor over the stove will greatly reduce the unwanted diffusion of odors and dirt.

The upper right photo shows a particularly harmonious kitchen setting, with an appropriate balance of elements. The sink area is illuminated by natural light from the window.

THE FIVE ENERGIES

Food is energy. As it grows and changes form, it passes through a cycle of transformation. Each phase corresponds to one of the fundamental energy patterns known as The Five Energies.

The Five Energies are given the names of five natural elements: Fire, Earth, Metal, Water, and Wood.

Fire shoots upward. It is energy at its most powerful, radiant like the brilliance of the sun. Earth energy moves in a horizontal, circular direction, just as the planet turns on its axis, creating stability and balance. Metal energy moves inward, becoming ever more intense. Water energy descends, the point in the cycle of maximum rest and concentration. It is like the new moon, dark and about to give birth. Wood symbolizes expanding energy, growing outward like a tree.

The system of the Five Energies is a way of understanding the fundamental processes of nature, and the way in which these work together to create a world of profound harmony. The art of eating well enables us to see these energy patterns as they manifest in the process of cultivation, transportation, preparation, cooking, and eating. Understanding this system helps us to see how even the most mundane tasks, like washing and chopping vegetables, fit into a far larger cycle of energy. If that cycle, and all the small details it embraces, is respected, the results can be wonderful. If the energy of any phase of the cycle is disturbed, we suffer the consequences.

EARTH ENERGY
Everything we eat grows out of the soil of our planet or, like livestock, is nourished by its abundance.

WATER ENERGY
Water is the energy of transport. No matter what its final destination, everything is taken on a journey from the fields.

METAL ENERGY
This is the phase of preparation. Almost everything we eat is prepared in some way before it is cooked or eaten. It gets cleaned, threshed, kneaded, chopped, sliced. Often it changes beyond recognition.

WOOD ENERGY

The characteristic of Wood energy is to expand. In this final phase, the nourishing power of the meal literally expands outward into the family and friends who consume it. It is literally transformed into the vital energy of human beings.

FIRE ENERGY

In this phase the food undergoes an even more profound transformation. This is the rite of purification. Old impurities are burnt away and new, more intense energy is added.

This sequence presents the most beneficial aspects of the cycle of food transformation. The ingredients are grown naturally. They are transported directly from farm to market to ensure freshness. They are prepared by hand, using simple utensils. They are cooked in ways that preserve their vital essences while increasing their energy. They are eaten in a harmonious setting.

These ways of handling food, while still found in many homes throughout the world, are no longer universal. Other influences now seriously affect the way food is grown, harvested, marketed, prepared, cooked, and eaten. Animals and vegetables are produced in unnatural environments. The food products are frozen, flown or transported across vast distances, from one season to another.

Then they are repacked, chemically altered with additives and preservatives, precooked, and changed in other ways that affect the essential qualities of the original food. In busy households food is cooked using methods and equipment that drain off whatever goodness remains and then hurriedly consumed by today's stress-ridden workers and their families.

KITCHEN ENERGIES

Kitchens are fascinating to us because we are drawn to their energy. All the Five Energies – Fire, Metal, Earth, Water, and Wood – are present in even the humblest of kitchens.

Associated with each of these energies are various qualities or vibrations that we experience every day – colors, smells, and tastes. Those energies are also manifested in various types of food.

In traditional Chinese culture, the system of the Five Energies was also used to interpret the significance of seasons, numbers, and directions. In traditional Chinese medicine, each of the twelve principal meridians, or energy pathways, of the body and its corresponding internal organ was classified according to one of the Five Energies. The correspondences between the energy patterns in food and herbs could be used in the treatment of imbalances in the body's energies.

The vibrations of the Five Energies interact with each other in cyclical patterns. The processes of nature involve patterns of energy which are perpetually rising, expanding, condensing and descending, with a period of transition when the direction of energy changes from one phase to another. This constant force of transition is the horizontally rotating energy of Earth.

WOOD
Most traditional kitchens have a great deal of Wood energy. Much of the kitchen furniture, worktops, and storage cupboards would have been fashioned of wood, and even if their function would be that of the supporting Earth energy, they would also exhibit the qualities of Wood. Certain types of nuts, such as hazelnuts and walnuts, are regarded as having the essential properties of Wood energy.

WATER
Water takes a number of forms in the kitchen. Apart from the obvious water system piped in to the sink and also to any other washing appliances, all other liquids in the kitchen are regarded as having the essential features of Water energy. This includes bottled beverages, including alcohol. Juicy fruits and melons are the foods whose energy is most clearly associated with that of Water.

METAL

Metal energy in the kitchen is easily identified whether it takes the form of steel, copper, aluminum, silver, or various other metals and alloys. Without Metal energy, we would have trouble cutting, chopping, mixing, grating, and any number of other tasks we take for granted in preparing meals. Among foods, spinach is a classic source of Metal energy.

FIRE

There is fire in your kitchen, whether or not you cook with gas. Electricity itself is Fire energy. Therefore all appliances that run on electricity manifest that power, regardless of their function. The Fire power of the modern kitchen greatly exceeds that of anything in the past. The arsenal includes the electric stove, microwave, food processor, toaster, coffee maker, refrigerator, freezer, light bulbs, dishwasher, and virtually any other piece of equipment. Among the foods stored in the kitchen, the torch of Fire energy is carried predominantly by red chilies!

EARTH

It is possible to see the kitchen itself as the Earth energy of your home. It is the place where all nourishment is stored and prepared. It sustains everyone in the household. It accommodates everyone who enters and absorbs the imprint of countless activities. Within the kitchen, the table, work surfaces, and chopping boards are all considered manifestations of Earth energy, regardless of the materials of which they are made. Glassware, being made of sand, manifest this energy as do pottery, tiles, and earthenware containers. Rice and vegetables are the primary foods associated with Earth energy.

THE EPICENTER

The center of your kitchen is the stove on which you normally cook your meals. This is the determining point for the correct arrangement of your kitchen. In Feng Shui this point is treated with the respect traditionally reserved for the family hearth. It is often considered the heart of the entire home.

The drawing of the topography will be familiar to you from the kitchen landscape introduced on pages 42–3. The animals are arranged according to their symbolic correspondence with the key points of the landscape – the tortoise to the rear, the dragon above and to the left, the tiger low down to the right, the phoenix flying ahead in front.

There is a significant difference, however, which is essential to understanding the Feng Shui layout of your kitchen. The central serpent is no longer facing forward toward the phoenix. The serpent has turned completely around and is facing the other way. This is because the serpent's central position has been taken by the hearth. In other words, your stove is now considered to be at the center of the entire landscape. Everything will now be determined in relation to it.

Thus, as you will see when we examine the various aspects of your kitchen in detail, your stove needs a solid wall or tortoise behind it. It needs space in front of it: this space will be its phoenix aspect where you, the cook, will work. High storage cupboards or tall pieces of equipment will find their natural position on the left (dragon) side of the stove. To the right (the tiger side) you will place smaller items, like a low cupboard.

You can use this plan to place all the various furnishings and equipment in your kitchen. Once that is done, however, you will still remain the wise serpent and just as in the original configuration of the Five Animals, you too will require a strong tortoise to your rear. Hence the advice you will find later in these pages about how to arrange the doorways and spaces behind you for maximum support.

DOORS AND WINDOWS

Your kitchen is a volatile environment. In many homes, no other room contains so many pieces of equipment, so many sources of energy, and so many potential risks. Keeping the basic atmosphere of your kitchen stable is therefore of prime importance in ensuring a safe and secure location in which to prepare meals. The location of doors and windows and their design plays a key role in protecting and stabilizing the space in which you cook. If they are appropriately positioned, your home, your food, your health, and your family will prosper. The examples on these pages will help you avoid some of the most common problems.

If the kitchen door is directly behind you when you stand at the stove, your back is unprotected. You have no tortoise. Even if you are cooking on your own, your nervous system will be alert to the fact that your back is exposed. This underlying tension will contribute to a sense of unease at a time when you should be calmly concentrating on your cooking. If you cannot change the position of your stove, make sure you close the kitchen door before you start to cook.

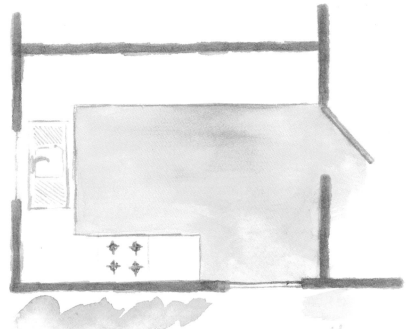

It is best for kitchen doors to open outward. By opening outward the doors effectively give priority and greatest protection to whoever is carrying hot dishes from the kitchen out to the dining table. This is one of the best ways to help prevent burns and scalds which can happen if there is a collision caused by someone entering the kitchen just as the food is being served.

If your kitchen has two doors which face each other, a turbulent stream of energy will be created if the two doors are open at the same time. Generally speaking, both doors should be closed, especially when food is being prepared and cooked. If you need extra ventilation and don't have an extractor fan, it is preferable to open one of the doors and the kitchen window. As shown bottom right, the flow of energy in the kitchen is likely to circulate in a comfortable circle, stimulating but not disturbing the space.

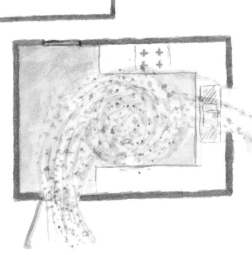

DOORS AND WINDOWS

The cooking element has been placed immediately in front of the window. This arrangement violates one of the fundamental principles of Feng Shui. The stove is the modern version of the hearth. It should be respected as a significant force in your home. It needs a strong tortoise at its rear. Its back should be against a solid wall, not a window. If the window is opened, draughts from outside will disturb the flames if you use gas and will dissipate the heat as you cook.

Some kitchens are equipped with swing doors. These look attractive and give the impression of making life easier for the busy cook who also has to serve the meal. But from the Feng Shui point of view, swing doors are an accident waiting to happen, particularly if there is more than one person involved in cooking, serving or cleaning up. If you have swing doors, either replace them with a one-way door or put in large windows to help prevent traffic accidents.

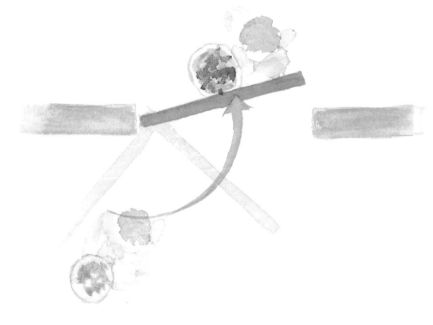

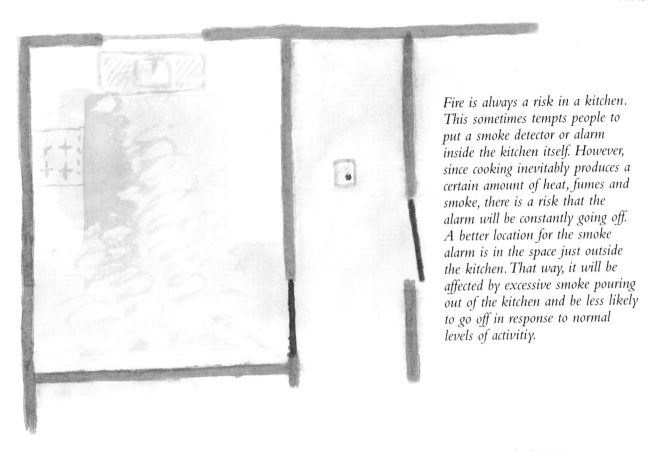

Fire is always a risk in a kitchen. This sometimes tempts people to put a smoke detector or alarm inside the kitchen itself. However, since cooking inevitably produces a certain amount of heat, fumes and smoke, there is a risk that the alarm will be constantly going off. A better location for the smoke alarm is in the space just outside the kitchen. That way, it will be affected by excessive smoke pouring out of the kitchen and be less likely to go off in response to normal levels of activitiy.

Some contemporary kitchen designers recommend installing glass doors in the kitchen. But it is important always to think about the safety aspect of the fittings in your kitchen. In the event of fire, large sheets of glass are likely to explode and shatter in the pressure and heat of the flames. Doors designed with small glass panels are likely to be far safer in a fire, as are doors with single porthole-style windows.

LIGHT AND AIR

Our ancestors cooked in the open air, benefiting from earth's natural conditions of light and space. Even though we now cook in enclosed spaces, we still need to pay attention to the quality of the light and air. The source of natural light in this kitchen is the window. It is correctly positioned over the sink where, during daylight hours, it is perfect for the clarity we need when washing vegetables, cleaning other foodstuffs or washing up.

We have long since left behind the days when we cooked and ate only when daylight permitted. A wide range of electric lighting is now manufactured for use in kitchens. Spotlights are increasingly popular as a designer installation, but they throw strong focused beams and produce a great deal of heat. If you have these in your kitchen, be sure to keep food away from them. Neon lighting is preferable because it uses the least amount of energy and generates the lowest amount of heat. Its subtle flicker, which could be a problem in a study or other areas of the house, does not have an adverse affect in the highly energized kitchen environment.

If you have a window that faces south, it will be best to have a washable blind that can be drawn on sunny afternoons. That will cut down on glare in the kitchen and help to control the temperature. This is particularly important if you are storing fresh vegetables or other items in the kitchen that could be affected either by too much sun or heat.

Keeping the air fresh in the kitchen is a constant challenge. You may be tempted to open the window, but that is not ideal when preparing and cooking a meal. You are exposing the food and utensils to external influences that may carry infections and invisible pollutants. Gusts of air can cause the kitchen temperature to fluctuate and disturb the atmosphere. Try to install an extractor fan directly over the stove — this will remove fumes and vapors almost as soon as they are produced, preventing them from diffusing and settling on the kitchen's work surfaces and equipment.

WATER WISDOM

In the classical Chinese book of divination, the *I Ching*, water is associated with difficulty. Its energies are very powerful and far from predictable. If there is one piece of advice consistently given by Feng Shui masters, it is this: take great care with water. You are advised, for example, not to live in a house that has a body of water at its back. The Water energy can be disturbing in a number of ways, producing health problems and sexual disorders. Any body of water to the rear of a dwelling weakens the all-important strength and support that should be given to the house by its tortoise.

We need water in the kitchen and because of its unique powers its position is important. This is best determined in accordance with the system of the Five Energies (see pp. 48–51). The movement of Water energy is exactly the opposite to the movement of Fire energy. Water energy descends; Fire energy rises. They are like constant enemies and whenever they struggle, explosive energy is released. The surging power of steam is released when fire overpowers water and brings it to the boil. Intense energy radiates outwards in all directions when firefighters turn their hoses on a burning building. The wise cook learns to control the interactions of Fire and Water energies and, unless absolutely necessary, keeps them separate in the kitchen.

The best arrangement for the contemporary kitchen, which will also meet the wishes and needs of most plumbers, is to group all the equipment that relies on water together in the same corner, or along the same wall. This would include not only the sink, but the washing machine, dishwasher, and any water purification system. The Water corner or wall should be opposite the area of the kitchen where you have the Fire energy of your stove and electrical food preparation appliances.

If it is not possible to have the Water energy and Fire energy on opposite walls or corners, then the next best arrangement is to have them at right angles to each other. The main principle to respect is never to put them side by side lest, like racing camels, they begin to fight.

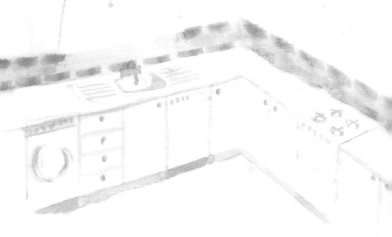

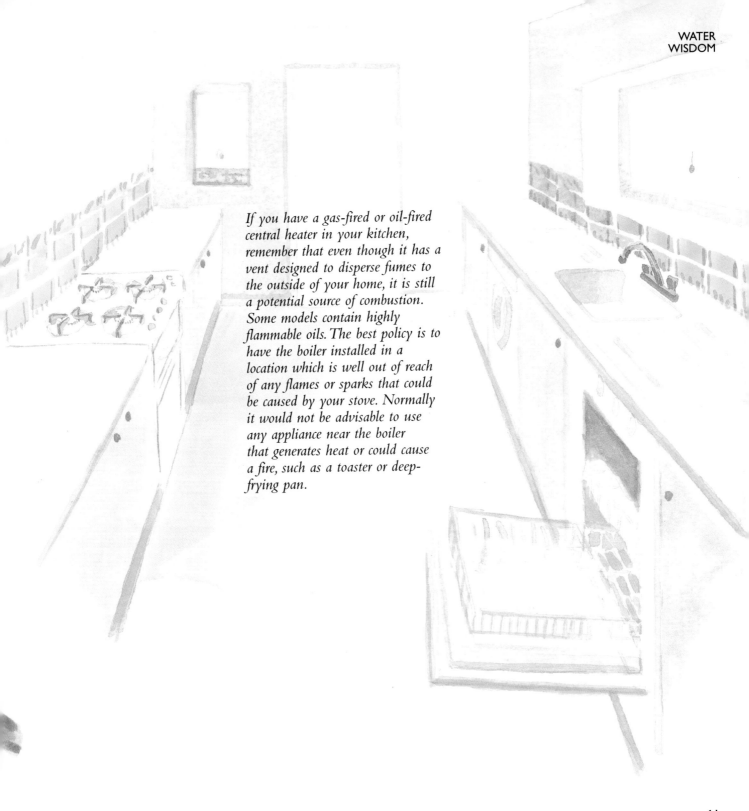

If you have a gas-fired or oil-fired central heater in your kitchen, remember that even though it has a vent designed to disperse fumes to the outside of your home, it is still a potential source of combustion. Some models contain highly flammable oils. The best policy is to have the boiler installed in a location which is well out of reach of any flames or sparks that could be caused by your stove. Normally it would not be advisable to use any appliance near the boiler that generates heat or could cause a fire, such as a toaster or deep-frying pan.

FIRE ENGINES

All electrical appliances have the power of
Fire energy. In the system of the Five
Energies (see pp. 48–9), this is the explosive,
upward rushing force of energy at its zenith.
It is this immense power that gives heat in all
its forms, including electricity, the ability to
bring about such rapid transformations when
it comes in contact with virtually anything
else in the natural world. Fire melts metal. It
bakes earth. It consumes wood. It boils water.
Its power can even be used to burn out
other fires.

Electricity has the same power. We recognize
that when the night sky is lit up with
lightning or when huge generators are
brought in to provide the power at an
open-air concert. However, in our daily lives
electricity tends to be taken for granted. All
electrical appliances, including wiring, have
electrical and magnetic fields associated with
them. Some may be of low power, but if you
create an environment entirely enclosed
within these fields or, worse still, spend your
days working inside one, as do many office
workers, you are exposing yourself to a level
of energetic disturbance that can negatively
affect your health.

We need this power in the kitchen. Properly
positioned and used, it is not harmful and we
can use its energy to enhance the value of the
food we eat. The best Feng Shui advice is to
allocate a specific area of your kitchen to this
energy. This will avoid creating too intense a
field all around you.

*The illustration on these pages
shows an arrangement with all the
electrical appliances arranged along
one wall. These include the stove,
toaster, electric kettle, microwave,
and food processor. Note that they
are at right angles to the wall
where the Water energy of the sink
and dishwasher is located. Even
though an appliance such as a
dishwasher needs electrical power, it
is treated as a Water energy device.*

If you have a small, low
refrigerator, you would normally
place it on the Tiger side of the
stove. A tall refrigerator/freezer
would be positioned on the
Dragon side.

SURFACING

WINDOWS

The most practical covering for your window is a washable blind. Ordinary fabrics and drapes will be continually soiled by airborne grease and vapors.

WORK SURFACES

The best materials for work surfaces are wood, marble, and formica or aborite. These are strong, resilient, and easy to clean. Ceramic tiles are unhygienic as a work surface because dirt and residue can accumulate in the minute cracks where the tiles meet. However, tiles are excellent for surfacing the walls around the areas where food is washed, chopped, and cooked. They are fireproof, easy to clean, and relatively low cost. Although stainless steel is increasingly fashionable, it is not considered appropriate in a home, either for a work surface or as wall protection. Although it is washable and fireproof, the steel holds heat which can prove dangerous and will certainly affect food stored in the kitchen. It should be reserved for properly regulated professional use in large kitchens.

WALLS

Wallpaper in the kitchen tends to peel off as a result of the humidity, steam, and changing temperatures. Wood paneling is attractive, but should be used elsewhere in the home where the risk of fire is low. Water-resistant, washable paint works best on the walls. The kitchen environment should be as calm as possible to provide an accommodating container for the many energies involved in preparing and cooking food. White, beige, and pastel shades are recommended colors.

CEILINGS

A wooden ceiling is a fire risk, particularly in a kitchen. Polystyrene tiles should be avoided for the same reason. Textured plasterwork collects smoke particles and is hard to clean. Plain, painted plaster is simplest and safest. Paint it white or use a pastel shade. Avoid dark colors overhead.

CUPBOARDS

The decor of your cupboards should be compatible with the overall emphasis on simplicity. Light-colored wooden cabinets work best. Try to avoid metal cabinets as their energy is too intense for neutral food storage.

EARTH WORKS

Earth tones work well in creating a nurturing work atmosphere in the kitchen. Light browns, beige, and yellow are welcome. Use a darker brown tone for the flooring.

DECORATION

The less the better. The best decoration in the kitchen is a fire extinguisher and a fire blanket.

FLOORS

Wooden floors are fine in a kitchen. Cork strips or tiles are inexpensive and work well as they yield slightly under pressure. When properly sealed they are easy to clean. Although slate and ceramic tiles are popular in designer kitchens, they tend to be cold and slippery and glasses or plates will shatter if you drop them. Good quality tile-patterned linoleum is preferable.

EATING OUT

Look at this poor fellow who is already hard at work early in the morning and doesn't take time for a decent breakfast. He has brought his laptop computer along with him and has set up his office on the counter. It doesn't take a medical specialist to know that eating and working are two completely different functions. You can't go on day after day mixing them up together without injuring your health. Just look at the place he has chosen for his lonely meal. He sits facing a wall of metal and is eating off a shiny chrome counter. Every surface is reflecting heat and light. No matter what is on the grill, the customer gets fried in this inferno as well. From the Feng Shui point of view, his back is also in trouble. It is completely unprotected, further contributing to his fundamental unease in life.

Contrast this solitary diner with the restaurant filled with people on the facing page. Everything is devoted to serving and eating a convivial meal. The seating arrangement is such that everyone is acting as a tortoise for someone else. The round tables stress the social aspect of coming together for a meal, even the assortment of dim sum on the rotating tray in the center of the table is designed for communal eating. Enjoyment comes first here.

That's also the message of the shop front of the Cantonese restaurant shown in the small inset. The owner has put all his delicacies out on display – octopus, goose, Chinese sausage, and shellfish. The sheer profusion, right down to the stacks of plates and chopsticks, carries the message that everyone is welcome and the more the merrier.

STORING

The earth is a vast storehouse. It holds the seeds of everything to which it gives birth. It holds everything that creatures need for their nourishment. It receives everything that is returned to it.

Your kitchen, like the earth itself, is a storehouse. A well-stocked kitchen holds all the basic staples. Its cupboards and racks are filled with dried herbs, spices, and seasonings. It also needs to keep fresh produce, fresh dairy products, and newly baked breads.

In classical China, a storeroom was specially created next to or beneath the kitchen. Foods could be safely stored away from the heat of day and the rays of the sun. The farming communities learned very early on that vegetables would stay fresh far longer if they

remained in direct contact with the earth from which they came. So the tradition developed of laying them out on the floors of the peasants' storehouses.

We can apply this wisdom today. The ideal storage facility is a small separate room or large walk-in cupboard adjacent to the kitchen. In some houses, it can be a space set aside in the basement. If possible, it should have a few little windows, be free from damp and have ceramic tiles on the floors and walls. Vegetables can be stored on the floor. You will find that they keep far longer this way than they do in the dampness and extreme cold of a refrigerator. Dry foods can be kept on racks near the windows, but out of any sunlight.

The idea of a separate food storage area is not unique to Chinese culture. Many people have developed similar systems. The pantry or larder was an essential part of homes constructed in Europe and North America until recently.

EARTH STORAGE

Earth energy is ideal for storage. This includes clay, porcelain, or earthenware containers and those made of glass. These have the advantage of being cool and dry on the inside. Earth energy is fundamentally calming and protective. Foods stored in these containers are less likely to be infected and rot. Foodstuffs that are best stored in the dark, such as sugar, salt, and pepper, can be kept in pottery or earthenware containers. Those that can be exposed to light, such as pickles, dried noodles, and nuts, can be stored in glass containers.

WOOD

Wooden containers, including those made of bamboo, are wonderful because they allow the passage of air. Products that need to breathe, like tea and cereals, keep at their best in wooden or bamboo containers. Products that go moldy if stored in metal, like cakes and breads, will also stay fresher longer in wood.

FIRE AND METAL

Plastic, being an oil extract, exhibits the energy patterns of Fire. All steel, aluminium, and similar containers manifest Metal energy. Neither is suitable for storage. Top quality plastic is so firm that it has qualities similar to earthenware and may be used, but ordinary cheap plastic is of very poor quality. It is hard to seal, its odor is picked up by almost everything that is stored in it and it makes cheese and other living products sweat. Metal energy has a heavy, condensing quality to it and creates a field of pressure inside a container. Metal energy interacts with many types of product. The food picks up traces of the metal and the metal itself starts to degrade.

69

SINGLE ROOM LIVING

Suppose you don't have a separate kitchen but live in an apartment or studio where you must accommodate a number of functions in a relatively open space. You can still apply the basic Feng Shui principles.

The examples shown on this page graphically demonstrate how they can be used whether you are a tenant living in a tiny room or someone whose home is an open-plan penthouse.

The tenant of this one room has a bed and clothes cupboard that take up most of the space along two walls. At the foot of the bed there is a washstand with running water. In the remaining space there is room for a table and chair. This table doubles as a tiny work space and a mini-kitchen. Various food containers are stored on the shelf under the table and there is a cooking element on top.

The tenant has very few options. One possibility for improving the internal dynamics of the room is a moveable screen. It can be placed, as shown in the plan, around the corner of the table. This will protect that area of the room from energy which intrudes when the door is opened. It also serves to create a barrier between the cooking element and the bed. Putting it in this position before going to sleep would be particularly helpful, as it will confine the Fire energy to that corner of the room. The room has already been skillfully arranged so that the Fire energy is on one wall, opposite the Water energy. The bed is safely tucked into the corner so that there is a solid tortoise behind the headboard.

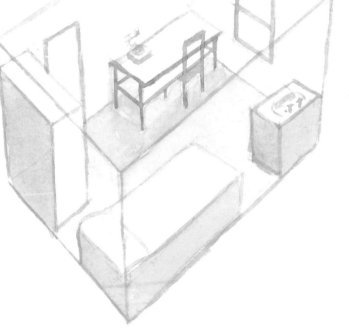

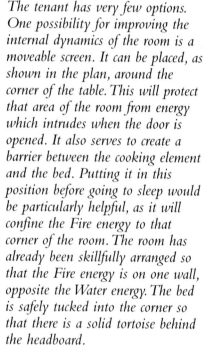

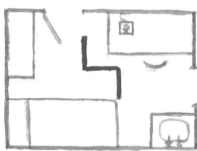

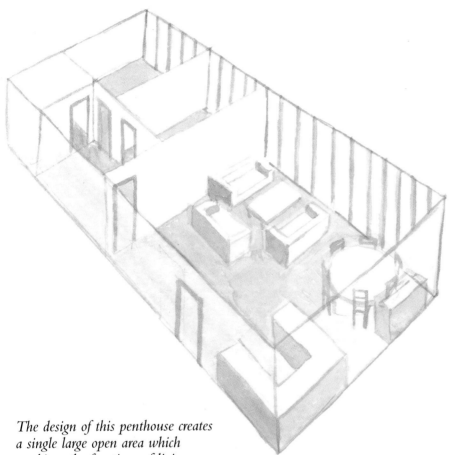

The real solution is to complete the kitchen space. This could be done by putting in the missing walls, or using floor-to-ceiling dividers with a folding door to save space. Whether or not that is possible, the age-old folding screen will come in handy here, too. A large screen is shown in the plan where it is used to create a "wall" around the sofa area so that its space is defined and protected. It could also be used to screen off the dining area. While it will not completely solve the problem of the exposed kitchen, it could be used to create a useful boundary around the missing sides of the kitchen space. This would at least create a proper container for much of the energy in the kitchen and go a long way toward shielding the rest of the open living space from it.

The design of this penthouse creates a single large open area which combines the functions of living room, dining room, and kitchen. The kitchen work surfaces, cupboard, and facilities are all fitted into one corner – so that the kitchen area itself really amounts to only half a room. That means that whoever prepares the meal, as they face the sink, the work surfaces and the stove, has no tortoise at their back at all. Furthermore, the rest of the open space is totally exposed to whatever energetic and atmospheric disturbance is caused by the cooking.

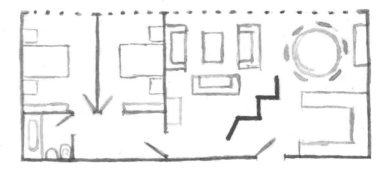

Preparing

AND COOKING

PREPARING AND COOKING

In spite of the incredible sophistication and variety in her cuisine, the Chinese cook owns few cooking implements, but relies instead on traditional skills, a knowledge of ingredients, and an intuitive grasp of how to balance tastes and textures to produce satisfying and nourishing meals.

Chinese cooking includes many styles. The most distinctive methods – stir-frying and steaming – are featured in this book. The recipes use ingredients which are relatively easy to obtain in a large Chinese supermarket. In most cases these foodstuffs – or appropriate alternatives – are found in most food shops.

Part Three begins with a brief description of the basic tools used in Chinese cooking – the cleaver, wok, and steamer – with instructions about their use and maintenance. You are then introduced to the basic principles of a balanced diet and taken on a tour of the Chinese pantry stocked with the ingredients needed for the recipes in Part Four. You will also find advice on the fresh ingredients used in those recipes and a small range of others. The pages on rice and noodles include several recipes illustrating different cooking styles.

Chinese cooking may seem complicated at first, yet in many ways it is deceptively simple. There are few of the rules commonly found in many other cuisines. The focus is on the art of cooking rather than on precise measurements, quantities, and clock-watching. The Chinese cook can produce a huge number of dishes out of a small range of ingredients, and can make something out of almost anything.

As an art form, Chinese cooking can be both a relaxing and a fascinating activity. There are only two essential requirements. First, you should be ready to give the preparation and cooking your full attention. Second, the ingredients should be as fresh as possible and of the highest quality available. Your taste buds and tummy, and those of your family and friends who eat with you, will be the only judge of your results.

COOKING WITH HEART

The entire world of food is regarded as an energy cycle, just as the home and kitchen are fields of energy which affect the quality of the meals prepared in them. You, the cook, are an energy field in your own right. The quality of your own energy, your relative strength or weakness, your inner feelings of relaxation or anxiety, also influence food as it is being prepared and cooked.

This is a novel idea to those who have only been exposed to the notion that cooking is a mechanical process that can be done successfully by following a series of step-by-step instructions. To the Chinese mind, cooking is more akin to the art of calligraphy. The calligrapher has a vivid idea of the characters that are to be written, but relies on the power of the moment and the quality of his or her internal energy to produce the required brush strokes. Indeed, it is in the very nature of the art that the calligrapher's state of mind is immediately evident in the lines made by the ink as it flows on to the rice paper.

So too with cooking. Food absorbs and reacts to the state of your energy. The relationship between you and the ingredients as you wash them, chop them, stir-fry them, and serve them is one of real intimacy. If you cook with a relaxed feeling of kindness and generosity towards those you are feeding, that penetrates the food as you handle it and work with it.

If you have followed the Feng Shui advice in the first half of this book, your kitchen will already be arranged in order to protect the cooking area from harmful energies and you will feel less nervous and more comfortable when you are cooking. If you follow the advice in this part of the book about food preparation, you will start to feel more in tune with the food you are working with and your attention will tend to be more focused on what you are doing in the kitchen.

Your cooking will also be helped by trying to bear in mind the oft-repeated saying that you are what you eat. The sage Kwan Tse said: "To the ruler, the people are Heaven; to the people food is Heaven." These words are based on a whole vision of society and can be understood in many ways. They reflect, in part, the understanding that it is from our daily food and drink that we derive the vital energy which not only supplies our bodies with sustenance, but also influences our entire spirit in profound ways.

CHOPSTICKS

It is natural to want to eat Chinese food with one of the most distinctive inventions of Chinese culture – chopsticks. They come in an astonishing array of materials. You can find chopsticks in gold, silver, ivory, jade, bone, lacquered wood, and bamboo. Bamboo chopsticks are probably the cheapest and easiest to clean. They are also less slippery. Normally, they are about 10 inches long.

Using chopsticks takes a bit of practice, but rapidly becomes second nature. They are held about a quarter of the way along from the thicker, upper end.

Rest one chopstick in the crook of your thumb, where the upper end of your thumb and index finger join your hand. The lower part of this chopstick lies across your third finger. Use the upper joint of your thumb to squeeze this chopstick firmly against this lower finger, so that it is held securely in place.

Now hold the second chopstick between the tips of your thumb and your first and second fingers, as if you were about to write with it like a pen or pencil. Use the flexible tips of your thumb and two fingers to move the topmost chopstick up and down over the stable lower one. Keep practicing until you get the feel of this pincer movement.

CLEAVERS AND BOARDS

Chinese cooks devote most of their time and skill to the careful preparation of food before it is cooked. When the ingredients for a stir-fry are placed in the cooking vessel, it takes only a few minutes to cook them. The real effort takes place beforehand.

A good cook devotes nine out of every ten minutes to preparing the ingredients and only the last minute to cooking. This extended preparation is practical as well as aesthetic.

The whole process from cleaning, through to soaking, cutting, and marinading has to be done first. Stir-frying and boiling are so fast that all the ingredients must be prepared and at hand before the pans are heated up.

If food is to cook evenly and quickly, then the individual pieces must be of a uniform size. The cook can then focus all of his or her attention on the art of cooking each ingredient to perfection.

Confucius observed that (one) "must not eat what has been crookedly cut." His advice has been heeded over the centuries.

The mosaic of harmonious shapes and integrated colors makes the dish pleasing to the eye. Without the effort of cutting everything up so evenly, the meal itself would be less harmonious. As it is, the dish can be easily and fairly shared.

When it comes to eating, the tradition of preparing small pieces eases the entire process, from the moment the morsels are picked up between the chopsticks and popped in the mouth until they are carefully chewed and digested.

This emphasis on preparation means that the Chinese cooking knife or cleaver has been developed into a multipurpose tool.

THE CLEAVER

The rectangular, flat blade of the cleaver is used for slicing, shredding, mincing, and chopping. Its unique features also make it perfect for crushing and scooping. The sharp corner of the blade is used to score lines into pork skin or squid, and to cut food into strips. The wide back can be used to pound and tenderize meat. The handle can be used as a pestle to grind spices.

The blade of the cleaver may be made from tempered carbon steel or high-carbon stainless steel, both of which are easy to sharpen. You need to dry a carbon steel cleaver carefully to prevent rust.

Most cleavers are fairly heavy, weighing between 4 oz. and 20 oz. The expert cook lets the cleaver's own weight do the work. It is lifted above the food and then allowed to slice naturally downward with a relaxed stroke, rather than pressed into the food. The choice of cleaver is a personal matter; it should rest comfortably in the hand, be well balanced, and feel like a powerful extension of your arm. If you are a first-time buyer, try starting off with a medium-sized cleaver.

Watching a skilled cook can be mesmerizing. Two cleavers may be used side by side for a large mincing job, thus halving the time needed. The action is so swift, it creates a continuous stream of energy. For the novice, all you need to learn are the basic skills shown on pages 78–9.

From the top: carborundum. The heaviest cleaver, size 1, is favored by professional chefs. Size 2, medium weight, is a good size for the novice. Size 3 is useful for delicate cutting.

Caring for your cleaver Keep your cleaver razor sharp. In classical China, and in many rural areas, this was the skilled work of traveling professionals.

A sharpening stone or carborundum is the tool for this job. It is worth trying to find someone who can show you how to do this properly, but following the instructions below will give you a good start. Buy a small stone that is rough on one side and smooth on the other. Use the rough side for blunt and damaged edges, the smooth for fine honing.

THE CHOPPING BOARD

Your chopping board is the Earth element which absorbs the shock and pressure of your cleaver. A traditional Chinese kitchen used a thick horizontal slice of tree trunk, both as a work surface and chopping board. It could be moved to wherever it was needed, inside the kitchen or outdoors. When the heavily used board developed an uneven surface, it was shaved down with the cleaver, leaving it good as new. Nowadays, the professional chef may use a board which is about 6 in. thick. For the contemporary home kitchen, choose a wooden board which is $1\frac{1}{2}$ in. thick and measures about 12 in. by 18 in. This size of board will stay stable while being used.

Clean the cleaver and sprinkle a few drops of oil or water onto the stone. Hold the cleaver firmly and rub the cutting edge gently on the stone, first away from you and then back toward you. Repeat this several times, then turn the blade over and sharpen the other side.

CLEAVER WORK

Slicing The simplest way of cutting food is to make thin, straight, parallel slices. This exposes a large area for quick cooking. Slicing is ideal for hard root vegetables and Chinese cabbage, as well as fish and meat. It can be easier to cut raw meat and fish into fine slices if it is partially frozen. Slicing across the grain of the long muscle fibers in meat helps to break them down for quick cooking and ensures that tough cuts become tender.

Grip the handle of the cleaver, allowing your index finger to rest on the side of the blade, giving greater control. Hold the ingredient with one hand and fold your fingers under. Using your middle knuckles as a cutting guide, slice straight down with the cleaver. Slide your knuckles back and slice again.

Diagonal slicing may be used with fish fillets or thin vegetables, like asparagus, leeks, or scallions, to produce a larger slice.

Shredding Meats may be cut into long slivers this way. Ginger and garlic are often shredded.

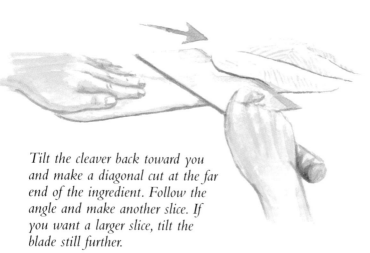

Tilt the cleaver back toward you and make a diagonal cut at the far end of the ingredient. Follow the angle and make another slice. If you want a larger slice, tilt the blade still further.

Slice the ingredient finely and stack the slices on top of one another. Using your knuckles as a guide, cut along the slice to produce long thin shreds.

Roll cutting This method exposes many surface areas and so speeds up cooking time. It works well with cylindrical vegetables such as carrots, asparagus, or leeks. It also allows each piece of a vegetable such as eggplant to have a little skin.

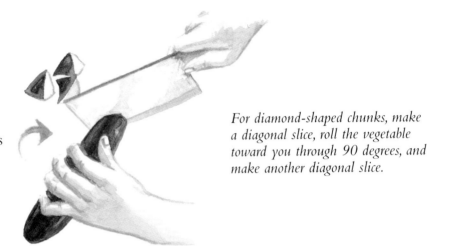

For diamond-shaped chunks, make a diagonal slice, roll the vegetable toward you through 90 degrees, and make another diagonal slice.

Chopping Large ingredients with fairly soft bones, such as fish, poultry, and spare ribs, may be chopped into small pieces this way.

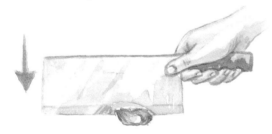

Hold the cleaver blade over the point where you wish to chop, lift the cleaver about 3 inches, and swing it down forcefully.

Mince chopping Use this technique for mincing meat, seafood, or vegetables.

Wet the blade of the cleaver to prevent the food from sticking to it. Cut the ingredient into small pieces and pile them up. Chop from one end of the pile to the other. Using the flat of the cleaver, scoop up the pile and flip it over. Repeat this process until you have a fine mince.

MARINATING, BLANCHING AND SOAKING

Before you start to cook, some ingredients need to be marinated, blanched, or soaked.

Marinating Meats and fish may need to be marinated. This process tenderizes and adds subtle flavors; it also gives a little protection against the fierce heat of the wok.

When marinating, always add the water and cornstarch, sugar and oil to the food first. Stir well, then add the soy sauce and salt. Five spice powder, ginger, garlic, or rice wine may also be added. The cornstarch dissolved in water will moisten the meat and provide a light protective coating against the salty ingredients which may toughen it.

Food can be left to marinate for just a few minutes, or for half an hour, or just the time it takes to prepare other ingredients. If left for too long the marinade may overpower the flavor and spoil the texture of the food. Vegetables are not usually marinated.

Blanching Plunging vegetables into boiling, salted water both cleans and sterilizes them. The tightly packed florets of vegetables such as broccoli and cauliflower may harbor germs and small bugs which cannot be washed out in the usual way. A few drops of oil are added to the boiling water, to help stabilize the color.

Soaking Dried, salted, pickled, or fermented ingredients may need to be soaked or reconstituted prior to cooking. It is a good idea to briefly wash the dried ingredients to get rid of dirt or debris, especially if you plan to use the highly flavored soaking water.

Dry products which are quickly steamed or stir-fried, such as dried Chinese mushrooms or tree fungus, need to be soaked overnight. If they are to be used in a long-cooked, braised, or stewed dish, 2 hours will be long enough. Dried shrimp need to be soaked for about 20 to 30 minutes before being cooked. The soaking liquid is full of flavor and can be strained and used in the final dish, if appropriate, or in soup or stock, or for cooking rice or noodles.

Salted and pickled ingredients may benefit from soaking to remove some of the very strong flavor and salt.

Bamboo leaves (see Jown, pp. 138–9) are always blanched to soften and sterilize them.

The three varieties of dried fungi (top) swell to different sizes when soaked (bottom) – from left: dried Chinese mushrooms, wood ears, cloud ears.

COOKING

Chinese cooking methods range across a spectrum that embraces the polar energies of Yin and Yang. All techniques are used – steaming, frying, braising, baking – depending on the local environment, the season, and individual health needs.

The only foods which are not cooked before being eaten are fruits. Cooking is the most reliable way of ensuring that the food is hygienic and free from bacteria. Stir-frying, boiling, and steaming are the most common cooking methods. They are toward the center of the spectrum of Yin and Yang, with boiling and steaming slightly more characteristic of nourishing Yin energy. Each method relies on intense, violent heat to achieve quick cooking.

The smoking hot oil conveys iron to the food, as well as sealing in the nutrients. Because of the intensity and fierceness of this heat, particularly when stir-frying, the best Chinese kitchens need to be regularly scrubbed down to remove all traces of smoke and grease.

Shallow-frying, deep-frying, barbecuing, and roasting are all very popular ways of cooking. The results are tasty, but the prolonged fierce, dry heat of the process tends to destroy many of the nutrients.

THE SPECTRUM OF YIN AND YANG

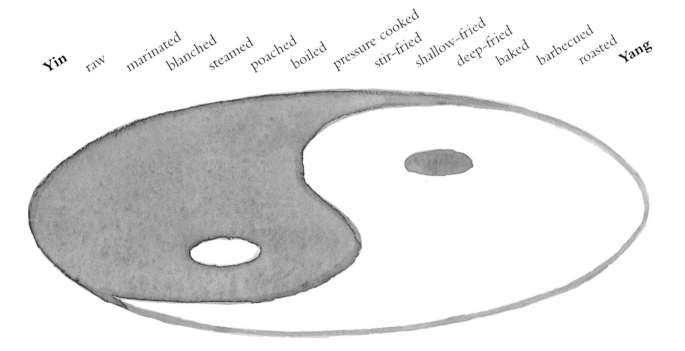

Yin   raw   marinated   blanched   steamed   poached   boiled   pressure cooked   stir-fried   shallow-fried   deep-fried   baked   barbecued   roasted   Yang

THE WOK

To cook the dishes presented in Part Four of this book, you will need a wok and a steamer. Ideally, it is best to cook over an open flame with instant control over the heat, so a gas stove is preferable.

THE WOK

A wok is a round-bottomed pan with sloping sides. The round bottom was originally designed for the traditional Chinese stove. Still used in some rural areas, these are solid structures inside which a wood fire is kindled. The round bottom of the wok fits snugly into a round opening on top, directly over the flame. Woks are made of iron, carbon steel, stainless steel, or aluminum. The traditional Chinese wok is made of iron or carbon steel. Both materials hold intense heat and conduct it quickly over the surface area. Both need to be seasoned (see right).

Woks and stoves If you cook with gas in your kitchen, a traditional wok with rounded bottom will be fine. You can also stir-fry on the solid hotplate of an electric stove, but it will not provide the fiercer heat and instant control of gas. Even in ultra-modern Hong Kong, people prefer to cook over the flame of gas.

Some cooks now use ultra-modern halogen stovetops, but although these offer instant heat control, their smooth flat surfaces are unsuitable for curved vessels like the wok. If you do use an electric stovetop or solid hotplate, however, it could be worth investing in a cast-iron wok with a flat base – a type which has recently appeared on the market. Or you could use a large frying pan with a heavy base and deep sides instead; this allows a large area to heat up evenly and quickly. In order to regulate heat more easily on an electric stove, turn two burners on at different settings so that you can move the pan from one to the other.

However, you should try to experience the thrill of using an authentic wok. So if your main stove has solid burners, it is worth buying a single or double gas burner run on bottled or canister gas. And if you happen to have a woodburning stove with a hole in the top, try using it!

Size of wok A 14 in. diameter wok is suitable for most family cooking. A wok with a single long handle is better for the novice cook than a two-handled one. The long single handle is usually heat resistant, so you can hold it while you toss the food, and hold a spatula in your other hand.

A wok is a multipurpose pan. As well as being good for general shallow-frying, a wok is excellent for deep-frying, as the relatively small quantity of oil that collects in the rounded bottom is in fact quite deep. If you buy a wok with a well-fitting lid, you can use the covered wok to poach, boil, braise, and steam food. A domed lid of 11 in. diameter, preferably with a wooden handle on top, will suit a 14 in. pan.

Seasoning and caring for your wok If you buy a traditional iron or carbon steel wok, you will need to season it before use. First wash the new wok in soapy water, giving it a good scrub to remove any machine oil used to coat the metal after manufacture. Dry the wok.

The traditional way to season a wok is using some fatty pork skin. Heat the wok, chop the skin into small pieces, and stir-fry vigorously in the wok for at least 5 minutes, preferably 10. Afterwards remove the skin and discard it, and wash the wok.

Another way is to brush a little vegetable oil over the entire inner surface of the wok. Place it over a low heat, increase the heat to medium and heat through for 10 minutes. Remove from the heat, wipe out with paper towels, and repeat the process once or twice. By this time your wok will have acquired a thin nonstick coating of oil that has been baked onto its surface. The wok is now ready for use.

Cleaning Boil some water in the wok and scour it with a hard brush, pour off the dirty water and dry the wok carefully. Don't use any detergent – it will remove the nonstick coating.

With regular use your wok will build up a good nonstick finish. Always dry it carefully. If it starts to rust, the surface will be destroyed. The easiest way to dry a wok is to place it over a high heat for 15 seconds.

Don't worry if the wok becomes blackened. This is the sign of a well-used wok. The modern obsession with shiny new surfaces can mean that people will be offended by the appearance of a black wok. If you must polish your wok, clean only the outside, but beware of rust.

WOK TOOLS

When you are in a Chinese supermarket you may see long-handled ladles, wire skimmers, and special long bamboo chopsticks. Some of these are for restaurant kitchens only, but there are simpler alternatives for home use.

LADLE A ladle is used for scooping up and stir-frying ingredients. In the home, a long-handled steel spatula can be used.

WIRE SKIMMER Traditionally used to lift food out of boiling water or when deep-frying, its open style allows the excess oil quickly to drip away. The wire soon becomes blackened with use, however, and is difficult to clean. This is not a problem in restaurant kitchens where frequent use means it is constantly being sterilized. For the home kitchen, a flat perforated stainless steel skimmer is a good choice.

CHOPSTICKS These make a cheap and effective whisk for sauces, for stirring beaten egg into soup or lifting ingredients. Their smooth surface makes them easy to clean and hygienic.

WOK STAND This keeps the wok balanced and steady on the stove. You will need one if you are steaming, braising, or deep-frying. A 10 in. diameter ring is the right size for a 14 in. wok. Choose a stand which is sturdy and has open sides. The open design allows heat to circulate freely and prevents the build up of any unburned gas.

STIR-FRYING

Stir-frying is wonderful for health. Thanks to the unique design of the wok, very little oil is needed. The smoking hot oil seals in the food's nutrients as well as producing a wonderful taste. The thin metal allows for sizzling, almost explosive heat underneath.

Stir-frying is the most famous of Chinese cooking techniques and the most difficult to master. The aim is to cook everything quickly and evenly with nothing overdone.

Choosing the right oil

It is best to use a light oil that will not burn, since the temperature inside the wok is unusually high. Extra virgin unrefined oils are unstable at high temperatures, and some oils have strong flavors which can overpower the natural taste of the ingredients. The best oils to use are refined sunflower, soy, vegetable, or peanut. Peanut oil is the favorite and produces a subtle smoky taste.

The basic approach

Heat the wok over high heat, add the oil, and swirl it around to coat as much of the wok's surface as possible.

When the oil is almost starting to smoke, add the ingredients according to the order given in the recipe.

Holding the handle of the wok, toss the food vigorously. Use the spatula or ladle to keep the small pieces constantly on the move. This rapid movement ensures that all surfaces of the food make contact with the sizzling hot wok and cook evenly without sticking or burning.

A lighter touch is needed when stir-frying fish, or the flaked flesh will break up into tiny fragments.

Flavorings, seasonings, and garnishes are normally added towards the end, to remain distinct from the flavors of the cooked ingredients.

Clockwise from top left: carbon steel wok stands on perforated wok stand, wok lid, stainless perforated strainer, traditional wire strainer, bamboo cooking chopsticks, spatula, and ladle.

Getting started

A stir-fried dish may be so simple that it consists of just one vegetable with a little seasoning to enhance its flavor or balance its energy (see Stir-fried spinach, p. 134 or Stir-fried greens, p. 154). Stir-fried onions is a favorite in the Lam household (see below). You can try any of these simple dishes to practice your technique. For more advanced stir-fry dishes see Potato pork, p. 142 and Singapore noodles, p. 149.

STIR-FRIED ONIONS
4 medium-sized onions
the green parts of 2 scallions, finely chopped
2 teaspoons oil
½ teaspoon Worcestershire sauce
½ teaspoon light brown sugar
a few drops of tabasco sauce

Peel and quarter or roughly slice the onions. Heat the wok over a high heat and add the oil, swirling it around to cover the surface. Add the onions and scallions and stir-fry vigorously for 3–4 minutes. Add the Worcestershire sauce and sugar and stir-fry for half a minute. Add the tabasco and serve immediately.

THE STEAMER

Steamed foods are traditionally prepared in bamboo steamers. These woven circular baskets stack one on top of the other, with a lid on the top. The wok is filled with boiling water and the bamboo steamer placed inside. The rounded bottom of the wok accommodates any size of steamer and the sloping sides make it easy to add extra water if needed.

Bamboo steamers are widely available and range in size from 4–16 in. in diameter. The small ones may be used for dim sum; the larger ones for fish or poultry. The beautiful handwoven design also makes the steamer a perfect serving vessel.

The right size Generally the steamer should be at least 2 in. smaller in diameter than the wok for stability and to trap enough steam under it for efficient cooking. You can wrap a clean teatowel around the base of the steamer to seal any gaps and ensure that the steam rises up through the bamboo baskets.

Some woks come with specially designed steaming racks (see facing page). These are useful for steaming large plates of food. They must be used with the wok lid on. Lifting a large plate of food out of the wok can be tricky, so look for a "mechanical hand" in a Chinese store. These ingenious devices have two or three adjustable arms, designed to fit different sized dishes or plates.

Caring for your steamer. To clean the steamer, boil some water in the wok, put in the layers and boil for 5 minutes. Remove and hang in an airy place to dry. Place a cabbage leaf or plate under the food you are steaming to prevent food from sticking to the bamboo weave and to make for easier cleaning.

STEAMING

Steaming uses wet heat, as opposed to the dry heat of an oven. Steam is a delicate cooking method. The moist heat preserves the texture, color and vitamins of food. If steam is used to cook breads and doughs, the results are light and soft. The moisture penetrates the dough and there is no hard crust.

With the exception of eggplant and tofu, vegetables are not steamed in China. Steam is wonderful for fish, however, leaving it tender and succulent. Freshly caught fish are always steamed; the rest are stir-fried.

Steam is also useful for heating precooked foods without drying them out.

Whatever you are steaming, remember these important points:

Don't try to cook food using more than two tiers of steamer at once. The heat in a third tier will not be intense enough for cooking. However, you can use three or four tiers to keep foods warm.

The water must be boiling before any food is placed in the steamer.

The boiling water must not come into contact with the food. The waterline should be about 1 in. below the level of the rack or bottom of the steamer.

Always keep the lid on the steamer.

Top left: wok with steaming rack stands on wok stand. A plate of food may be placed on the steaming rack and the wok covered with the wok lid. Right: 2-tier bamboo steamer and lid. Front: "mechanical hand" for lifting hot plates.

SHOPPING AND SNACKING

Food is central to much of Chinese life. It is an essential part of many social rituals and cultural events. Business deals are concluded over a meal and Chinese banquets are famous the world over.

Perhaps food is all the more appreciated because the Chinese know what it means to live with very little. They have learned to survive in harsh conditions that have included vast famines. Simple, often primitive living conditions have molded the food of China into what we see today. Many foods are dried, pickled, or salted so that they can be used under almost any conditions throughout the year.

Whenever possible, however, families and cooks aspire to shop every day for fresh ingredients, a deeply ingrained habit born of the need to find daily supplies in the absence of refrigeration or other forms of cold storage. Everyone tries to find the freshest foods. Some people go food shopping two or three times a day. No wonder that food markets continue to play a central role in the daily life of Chinese people everywhere.

Any market in the Chinese-speaking world will have food stalls offering a variety of fresh and dried snacks, as well as light meals. Street vendors sell soup, noodles, and steamed buns. These are the ancestors of the contemporary

take-out, catering to the Chinese love of snacks between meals.

In China, what people cook depends on where they live. There are great regional variations embracing a wide range of climatic conditions. As a result there is an extraordinary variety of ingredients in the country's cuisine – from a reliance on rice as a basic food in the south to the predominance of other cereals like wheat, millet, and barley in the cooler north. In Szechuan, with its humid climate, spicy food is common as a protection against illnesses caused by damp.

A Chinese supermarket is a world in itself. If you are unfamiliar with China, its culture and language, the supermarket may at first appear to be a strange land of colorful packets with indecipherable labels, mysterious foods in the freezers, and a bewildering array of cooking equipment and implements.

But there is a fundamental simplicity about Chinese cooking. Once you have mastered the techniques and understand how to put various ingredients together, it is easy to improvise and develop an instinctive approach to cooking. This simplicity is the door to your own creativity.

LIGHT AND SHADE

Foods which grow in the open air in full sunlight differ from those which mature within the earth or in the dark. Just as the Chinese characters for Yin and Yang show a hill in shadow and in sunlight, so are foods grown in those conditions understood to have the differing powers of Yin and Yang.

Animal products, including eggs, are normally regarded as Yang. They are often recommended for people whose health is poor and who suffer from a deficiency of Yang energy.

Fish are exposed to the sunlight that filters through to them in their watery kingdom. At the same time, they swim within the basins of the earth's oceans and rivers. They have a relative balance of Yin and Yang energies – and fish dishes are often included in the diets recommended for people with a deficiency of either form of energy.

Rice also has the quality of balanced energy. It grows in the sun, but the individual grains are sheltered from the rays by their husks. This moderate energy makes rice a perfect staple that can be combined with all diets and eaten the whole year round. Brown rice, as its reddish tones indicate, is more Yang than white polished rice.

The portion of vegetables that grow above the earth is normally Yang. The roots that develop within the soil are considered Yin. Thus, root vegetables such as sweet potatoes are Yin – as are beansprouts which grow in the dark – whereas the upper shoots of scallions are Yang.

Most fruit, even though it is filled with water, has matured for months in the air and direct sunlight. Its energy is characteristically Yang.

陽

陰

Beware of taking too simplistic an approach,
however. Some animal products are less
Yang than others. On the other hand,
ginger and garlic, which are roots, have
distinctively strong Yang energy. The expert
cook takes all these variations into account
when preparing a meal and these many
subtleties, too numerous to mention, are
fully reflected in the seasonal recipes in
Part Four.

91

THE CHINESE PANTRY

SOY SAUCE Light and dark soy sauces are used in marinades and stir-fries as well as for general seasoning. Soy sauce is made from fermented soy beans, wheat, and water. Sometimes salt, sugar and other flavorings, for example mushroom extract, are added. Dark soy sauce is fermented for longer than the light variety, and has a slightly sweeter flavor. It is used to add rich color. Light soy sauce tends to be saltier in taste. Both types keep indefinitely.

OYSTER SAUCE Made from extract of boiled oysters, and seasoned with soy sauce, salt and spices, it adds a savory flavor which is not "fishy" and is often used as a seasoning at the end of cooking beef noodles. Refrigerate after opening.

RED RICE VINEGAR This mildly flavored pale red vinegar is made from fermented rice and is far less acidic than most wine vinegars. Rice vinegar adds a subtle sourness to a dish or can be used as a dipping sauce. It is a very healthy food and its sour taste is especially beneficial in summer.

CHILI SAUCE There are many types of chili sauce, so experiment to see what kind you prefer. A small bowl of chili sauce can be served with the meal and may, according to taste, be added to soup or noodles or used for dipping dumplings.

FIVE SPICE POWDER This distinctive aromatic spice is a mixture of ground star anise, fennel seed, cloves, cinnamon, and ginger. It is used to flavor dishes while cooking and also in marinades (see Jown, pp. 138–9).

ROCK SUGAR As its name implies, this sugar comes in large crystals. Beautiful to look at

and lovely to use, it has a delicious, silky sweetness. If you cannot find rock sugar, use natural turbinade or light brown granulated sugar instead (see Dried bean curd with eggs, p. 135).

SLICED SUGAR (brown sugar in pieces) is partly refined into slabs which are then cut up. Resembling brown sugar and caramel in color, it is used in desserts (see Sweet potato soup, p. 125).

DRIED SHRIMP Salted and dried shrimp have a strong flavor. They are used in small quantities to add depth of flavor to soup, and to steamed, boiled, or long-cooked dishes. You can buy them in plastic packs in Chinese stores. Look for ones which have a good pink color – if they are grayish they are out of date. It is best to reseal the pack and store it in the refrigerator after opening. To reconstitute dried shrimp, soak them in hot water for at least half an hour, or overnight in a cool place (see Vegetable cake, p. 119).

DRIED MUSHROOMS

Dried fungi of all sorts feature in Chinese cuisine adding rich flavors, colors, and textures. They will keep for a couple of years in a screw-top jar and must always be soaked before cooking. To reconstitute dried mushrooms, put them into a small bowl of warm water and leave for at least 2 hours or overnight.

DRIED CHINESE MUSHROOMS are the most popular variety. All Chinese supermarkets sell them. You will find a wide range of sizes and prices – not surprisingly, medium-sized ones are the most popular. Especially prized are those with tortoiseshell crazing on the tops.

Clockwise from top left: sliced sugar, Chinese dried mushrooms, wood ears, cloud ears, dried shrimp, rock sugar.

These are chewy and, when cooked over a long period, develop a soft, resilient, almost meaty texture (see Chinese mushroom and chicken soup, p. 130).

CHINESE TREE FUNGUS There are two types of black mushroom – large ones, commonly called wood ears, and tiny ones, called cloud ears. The small variety are black on one side and furry beige on the other, and have a delicate, sweetish flavor. The larger wood ears are black on one side and white on the other; these are heathier and cheaper than the small variety. Wood ears remain slightly crunchy when cooked (see Hot and sour soup, p. 150).

FRYING OILS

Only oils that are stable at very high temperatures are used for stir-frying. The oil also needs to be light enough not to overwhelm the flavor of the ingredients. The best oils are peanut or corn oil. Otherwise you can use an ordinary vegetable, soy, or sunflower oil. Sesame oil is used for its fine flavor rather than as a cooking oil. This flavor is best appreciated by simply adding a few drops at the end of the cooking process. It is also used to add depth of flavor in dipping sauces.

FLOURS

CORNSTARCH Made from corn, cornstarch is used to thicken marinades and sauces. The sauce will be opaque, however, so if you prefer a more glossy, clear sauce, use arrowroot or potato flour instead.

RICE FLOUR Traditional white rice flour, sometimes called rice powder, is available in Chinese shops and other specialist stores. Much lighter than wheat flour and much easier to digest, it is gluten free.

WHEAT FLOUR All-purpose, bread, and self-rising white flours are used extensively in Chinese cooking to make pastries and breads. Some of these are steamed, pale in color, and soft in texture, others are deep-fried, brown, and crisp. Wheat flour is used to make the dough for dumplings (see p. 116). It is also used for noodles (see pp. 96-7) which, along with rice, form the mainstay of most Chinese meals. Wholewheat flour is not normally used in Chinese food.

RICE

Rice has been a staple food in southern China for at least 3000 years. The name for rice is "fan", the same as for meal. The greeting "Have you had rice?" is universal. Rice is eaten in the morning, at noon, and in the evening. Some people may eat up to 1 lb. of rice in one day. There are many varieties, including long grain, short grain, and glutinous.

LONG GRAIN RICE is the most commonly used. It is boiled or steamed to accompany other dishes. Leftover rice can be stir-fried to make dishes such as Egg fried rice (see facing page).

SHORT GRAIN RICE, found more in the north of China, is used for congee, a type of rice porridge eaten for breakfast (see pp. 128–9).

GLUTINOUS RICE, also known as sticky rice, has rounder pearl-like grains and must be soaked before cooking. It becomes very sticky when cooked and has a sweet flavor. It can be served on its own, cooked in lotus or bamboo leaves, or used for stuffings and desserts. It is also used for making wine and vinegar.

RED RICE, with its red husks, is used to make vinegar and, with soybeans, it is used to make red fermented bean curd.

Preparation Rice is always washed before being cooked, even when prepacked. Washing rice has become a ritual that signals the beginning of meal preparation. The required amount of rice is put into a shallow bowl and covered with cold water. The water is swished around with the hands until the impurities float to the surface. The water is then poured off, and the process repeated twice more. The rice is then drained and ready for use.

Cooking rice It is hard to give perfect instructions for cooking rice. The absorbency of the rice depends on the variety and where it was grown.

Here is a traditional Chinese method of gently steaming rice. Wash the rice, allow ⅓–⅔ cup per person, and drain it. For each cup of rice, allow 1¾ cups of water.

Put the rice into a large pan. Add the cold water, cover the pan, and bring it to the boil over a high heat. This will take about 5 minutes. Turn the heat to low and cook gently for about 20 minutes, until the water is no longer visible and small craters start popping up on the surface of the rice. Turn off the heat, leave the lid on the pan and allow the rice to finish cooking in its own steam. This will take about 10 minutes. Do not lift the lid during this final stage of cooking.

Never stir rice while it is cooking. You can fluff it up with a pair of chopsticks just before serving.

TOP TIP!

In China the second or third rinsing water may be saved and used to soak strong-smelling fish. The starchy water absorbs the smell; the fish is then rinsed before being cooked.

BOTH RECIPES SERVE **4** PEOPLE

CHICKEN, CHINESE MUSHROOM, AND SAUSAGE CASSEROLE

In this fragrant, substantial dish, the separate flavors of all the ingredients are gently absorbed by the rice. Traditionally, the chicken skin and bones are included; use boned, skinned chicken if you prefer.

2½ cups rice
1½ lbs. chicken thighs or boned chicken
2–3 small dried Chinese mushrooms
per person
1 Chinese sausage per person
½ in. grated fresh ginger root

marinade for the chicken:
2 teaspoons soy sauce
½ teaspoon salt
½ teaspoon sugar
2 teaspoons cornstarch dissolved in
2 tablespoons water

garnish:
chopped scallion

Wash the mushrooms and leave them to soak in a small bowl of warm water for at least half an hour, or overnight in cold water, if you prefer. Chop or slice the chicken into ½ in. pieces, remove the skin if you like. Cut the sausages into ½ in. diagonal slices. Wash the rice then tip it into a large, heavy-bottomed, lidded skillet or pot. Add sufficient cold water to cover the rice and come ¾ in. over the top of it. Bring the water to a boil and cook over medium heat until most of the water has been absorbed and little craters are starting to form on the surface of the rice.

Now put the sliced sausages, drained mushrooms, the chicken pieces, and the ginger on top of the rice. Cover the skillet tightly and turn down the heat as low as possible. Leave for 15 minutes or until everything is cooked. Now remove the skillet from the heat, garnish with the scallion, replace the lid, and allow the skillet to stand for another 10 minutes.

Serve the dish from the skillet, everyone will enjoy the wonderful aroma as you lift the lid.

EGG FRIED RICE

This is a delicious way to cook leftover rice.

3½ cups cooked rice
1 tablespoon oil
4 eggs
3 finely chopped scallions
2 teaspoons light soy sauce
salt to taste

Beat the eggs with a little salt. Heat the wok, add 1 tablespoon of oil and carefully swirl it around to cover the whole surface; this is important as it will prevent the rice from sticking. Stir-fry the eggs very briefly and remove to a plate. Reheat the wok, add the rice, and stir-fry until the grains are separated and hot. Add the scallions and stir.

Chop the eggs roughly and return them to the wok, stir in. Add the soy sauce and stir-fry for 30 seconds. Transfer to a heated bowl and serve.

NOODLES

Originally made in the north of China from all-purpose wheat flour, noodles are now popular all over the country and are also made from rice flour. They can be bought fresh or dried and come in many widths and thicknesses, from fine thread noodles to flat noodles ½ in. wide. If you buy more fresh noodles than you need for cooking, you can freeze the surplus.

To cook Allow about 8 oz. of noodles for 2–4 people, depending on everyone's appetites.

Bring a large pot of water to a boil, add the noodles and bring back to a boil.

Homemade noodles will need only 3–4 minutes, dried noodles 8–10 minutes depending on size, so follow the directions on the pack.

If you buy fresh egg noodles, cook them for 1 minute only, as they will already have been steamed. To test whether noodles are cooked, lift one out to check; it should be pliable and if you cut it, it should be the same color right through.

Unless you are making a noodle soup, rinse noodles in cold water after cooking and draining, then drain again before combining with other ingredients. If you have boiled them some time before making your dish, just rinse them again with cold water to separate the strands.

BOTH RECIPES SERVE **4** PEOPLE

HOMEMADE NOODLES

Even though there are noodles aplenty in every shop, it is worth making your own. You will be delighted with the texture and flavor of fresh noodles, even though the shape may not be perfect.

Use unbleached organic bread flour. You will need a large bowl, a large floured board or clean work surface, and a long rolling pin.

2 cups bread flour
I teaspoon salt
around ⅔ cup cold water
I tablespoon oil

Sift the flour into the bowl with the salt. Make a well in the center. Add 1 tablespoon of water and the oil. Using a pair of chopsticks, start to stir. Continue adding small amounts of water and keep stirring until most of the flour has formed into a large ball, not too sticky. Gather the dough up with your hands and place it on a floured board. Knead the dough by rhythmically stretching and punching it until it is smooth and elastic. The dough is ready if it bounces back a little when you push your finger into it. Cover the dough with a damp cloth and leave it to rest for an hour. When you are ready to make the noodles, put the dough on the floured board, and sprinkle a little flour on the rolling pin. Flatten the ball of dough into a circle and start to roll it out. As you roll, turn the dough occasionally to prevent it sticking to the board, adding more flour to rolling pin and board if necessary.

Take care not to add too much flour or the dough may get too dry and start to crack. When the dough is about ⅛ in. thick, but not so thin that you cannot lift it, sprinkle a little flour over the surface, and fold the dough over and over into a flat roll about 2 in. wide. Using a sharp knife, cut across the dough at ¼ in. intervals to form the noodles. Gently loosen the noodles with your fingers and allow them to air for a few minutes. Boil the noodles for 3–4 minutes.

NOODLE SOUP

This is a good dish for lunch, using your own homemade noodles or packaged noodles.

½ lb. noodles
¼ lb. pork
2 medium-sized dried Chinese mushrooms
4–5 small bunches (around 6 oz.) bok choy
I teaspoon oil
¼ teaspoon white pepper

marinade for pork:
2 teaspoons light soy sauce
¼ teaspoon salt
½ teaspoon sugar
I teaspoon cornstarch dissolved in
I tablespoon water

Wash the mushrooms to remove any grit and put them to soak in a small bowl of warm water for at least 30 minutes. Bring plenty of water to a boil in a large pot, add the noodles, bring back to a boil and cook until tender. Drain, rinse with cold water, and set aside to drain. Slice the pork thinly into slices about 1 in. long and put them into a bowl with the marinade ingredients, stir gently until they are coated.

Snap the leaves off the bok choy, wash them carefully and cut them crossways into strips.

Remove the mushrooms from their soaking water; trim off and discard the tough stems. Slice the tops thinly and add these, the soaking water, and 3 cups of water to a medium-sized pot and bring to a boil.

Add the marinated pork, bring back to a boil and cook for 4 minutes. Now add the noodles, the bok choy and the oil to the pot and bring back to a boil. Remove the pot from the heat, sprinkle the soup with a few drops of dark soy sauce and the white pepper; transfer to a heated bowl and serve.

Quick cooking means the bok choy will be very crisp. For softer bok choy, add it at the same time as the pork.

VARIATION

You can use chicken, beef, or shrimp instead of pork. These will need to be cooked for only 2 minutes, or until there is a distinct color change.
This soup, prepared without meat, is enjoyed by vegetarians in China. You can increase the amount of white pepper to warm you up.

BEANS AND BEAN PRODUCTS

Beans consist almost wholly of protein and are high in vitamin B$_1$. Each continent has its own native bean; China's is the soybean. This humble bean is one of the few complete vegetable proteins containing all eight essential amino acids. Most countries stew their beans or make them into flour, but in China, the soybean is used whole, sprouted, fermented, or dried.

Soybean flour is used in bread and baking, while the oil is used for cooking and in the manufacture of margarine. Soy milk – a nondairy product – is used in ice cream and to make tofu. Soybeans can be transformed into many varieties of bean sauce, as well as the more familiar soy sauce (see p. 92).

TOFU, or doufou (also known as bean curd), is made from ground yellow soybeans and water. Normally sold in small slabs, its texture is like a set custard. Tofu readily absorbs the flavor of whatever it is cooked in. One of the most versatile foods in the Chinese kitchen, it can be shallow- or deep-fried, braised, boiled, or steamed. It is high in protein yet low in fat and cholesterol. Tofu is found in many forms in different parts of China – sweetened, young, old, fermented, deep-fried, and countless others. In this book it is used in the following forms.

FRESH TOFU can be found on square wooden boards in Chinese supermarkets. It is also sold in vacuum packs, which keep for a long time in the refrigerator – check the pack's "use by" date.

FERMENTED BEAN CURD (often called "Chinese cheese") is sold in jars. These small cubes of bean curd may be white or red. The latter contains red rice and has a stronger taste. The white is also available with chili added. Used in small quantities, all types give an unusual savory flavor. (See Stewed bean curd with lamb, p. 152, Stir-fried spinach, p. 134.)

DRIED BEAN CURD SHEETS OR "SKIN" are made by skimming off the skin from large vats of simmering soybeans and water. The skins are gently lifted off and left to dry before being packed for use. The sheets may vary in thickness, very fine paper thin ones being dissolved to make custard, and thicker ones softened before being fashioned into vegetarian meats (see Dried bean curd with eggs, p. 135).

DRIED BEAN CURD STICKS The skin from vats of bean curd is pushed to one side before being lifted out and dried to form these thick wrinkled sticks. They are used in dishes which need a more substantial, slightly chewy texture (see Stewed bean curd with lamb, p. 152).

FERMENTED BLACK BEANS are black soybeans preserved in salt. They are very popular in modern Chinese cooking, and are the main ingredient in black bean sauce. Available in packets or bags, they should be washed before use. Chop or crush them with garlic or ginger before adding to a dish – this helps to release their unique, powerful flavor. When using these beans in a dish, reduce the quantity of salt or soy sauce. Placed in a jar with a screw top, they keep indefinitely. (See Eggplant with black bean sauce, p. 143.)

MUNG BEANS (GREEN BEANS) These tiny beans can be sprouted into bean sprouts and used in stir-fries. They are wonderful cooked whole; split mung beans are also used (see Jown, pp. 138–9).

FLOUR made from mung beans is used to make transparent (cellophane) noodles.

BEAN SPROUTS You can sprout your own mung beans. Take a handful of mung beans, rinse well in running water, and put into a tall jar. Cover them with water and leave to soak overnight. Next morning drain off the water by pouring the beans into a sieve. Put them back into the jar and put a thin layer of cheesecloth over the top of the beans. Put the jar into a warm, dark cupboard. Two or three times a day take the jar out of the cupboard, remove the cheesecloth, and rinse the beans with lukewarm water. The beans will sprout and be ready to eat in four to five days.

Once sprouted the beans should be rinsed well, drained, and kept in the refrigerator in a plastic bag for three to four days at the most. Growing your own beans is economical and provides you with the freshest of bean sprouts. You can also buy packets of fresh beansprouts in all large supermarkets and Chinese grocery stores. Avoid canned bean-sprouts, they are soggy and do not taste fresh.

ADZUKI BEANS (RED BEANS) These are tiny, like mung beans, and are often used in desserts. Red bean paste, made from sweetened adzuki beans, is used as a filling for steamed dumplings, cakes, and pastries.

Top half of picture – soybean products: clockwise from top left: fermented black beans, dried bean curd sheets, fermented bean curd, dried bean curd stick, fermented red bean curd, and, center, fresh tofu. Lower half of picture: green (whole mung) beans, bean sprouts, yellow (split mung) beans, red (adzuki) beans.

FRESH INGREDIENTS

GINGER It is said that Canton has three treasures – Mandarin (orange) skin, old ginger, and rice straw. Mandarin skin is used as a catalyst in many medicines, rice straw is used as a cooking fuel, in house building, and for making furniture. A most healthy and versatile food, ginger is traditionally used to balance Yin and Yang energy. It is therefore a common ingredient in Chinese cooking. Ginger soup is used to cure drunkenness, ginger syrup to treat fainting and for relieving trapped wind and reducing swollen body tissue (edema). New mothers are given ginger stir-fried with rice to aid their recovery.

The root of the ginger plant has a pale brown skin and cream-colored flesh. Look for smooth, unwrinkled skin. If you are lucky you may see young ginger for sale – it is white, tinged with pink, and looks very juicy. This young ginger can be eaten as a vegetable. It is also available sliced and pickled in jars (see Ginger and pineapple beef, p. 132). Ginger wrapped in plastic wrap will keep in the refrigerator for about two weeks.

To cook In stir-fried dishes, ginger can be sliced, shredded, peeled, or minced. When used as a flavoring in long-cooked dishes it is cut into ⅛ inch slices. It can be used in soup, with meat, fish, seafood, also in desserts, puddings, and cakes (see Egg pudding with ginger, p. 155). Ginger is an essential ingredient in stir-fried vegetables.

GARLIC This wonderful medicinal plant has been used in Chinese cuisine for centuries. Look for large, plump, papery, white-skinned bulbs. Ideally garlic cloves should have a pinkish skin. The cloves can be used whole, sliced, minced, chopped, or shredded. Store in a cool, dry, light place.

To cook Pull off some cloves. If you find it difficult to remove the skin, tap the clove lightly with the flat side of a cleaver or heavy knife. This will loosen the skin so that you can pull it off. Garlic is often combined with scallions, ginger, shrimp paste, fermented black beans, or chilies to create sauces. It is used in many stir-fried dishes.

SCALLIONS (OR GREEN ONIONS) These are young onions with a white bulb and long green tubular leaves. Both parts are used, often separately. Along with ginger and garlic they are the most frequently used fresh flavoring in Chinese cuisine. Look for scallions that have rich green leaves and are not wilted. They will keep in the refrigerator for 2 to 3 days.

To cook Trim off the roots and any damaged leaves. Wash thoroughly and use as directed. Scallions are often used in stir-fries, added right at the end so that they remain crisp and brightly colored, and retain their wonderful taste and smell.

CHILIES These fiery red pods come in a variety of sizes, from 1½ in. to 4 in. The hottest parts are the white inner ribs and flat yellow seeds. If you prefer, you can slice open the chili and remove these. Otherwise proceed with caution and use a very small quantity until you find out how much heat you can tolerate. Because they are so very hot, you must be careful to wash your hands, knife, and

board after handling them and make sure to avoid touching your eyes or lips.

To cook Wash and slice the pods thinly and add to soups (see Hot and sour soup, p. 150) or stir-fried dishes. Or they can be used whole to give heat to a dish, then removed before serving.

CILANTRO (OR CORIANDER LEAVES OR CHINESE PARSLEY) Cilantro looks like flat parsley but has a more pungent smell and taste. It is readily available in supermarkets as well as Chinese and other Asian stores. Look for dark green leaves. Any yellowing means it is not fresh. Wash it carefully and drain thoroughly, then wrap loosely in paper towel, put it into a plastic bag and store in the refrigerator. It should keep for several days.

To cook In Chinese cooking cilantro is used sparingly as a flavoring in sauces and stuffings or as a garnish. It is considered unhealthy when raw. In cooking it loses its pungent taste and smell and releases a light lemony flavor. It is regarded as the classic accompaniment to fish and seafood. (See Fish soup with cilantro, p. 140, Peace and well-being for young and old, p. 151.)

BOK CHOY, PAK CHOI This "Chinese cabbage" looks and tastes a bit like Swiss chard. The plant can grow up to 20 in. tall, but is usually harvested young at less than 8 in. You can also buy very young bok choy measuring less than 5 in. The dark green leaves are smoothly

From the top: garlic bulbs, large scallion, fresh cilantro, chilies, fresh ginger root, young ginger root, pickled young ginger.

rippled, the stems short, plump, and pearly white. The leaves are earthy and slightly sweet, the stems very crisp and juicy. Shanghai bok choy are of similar shape but are a soft pale green color overall. They are not as crisp as bok choy and need less cooking. Bok choy will keep in the refrigerator for about 3 days.

To cook Snap the leaves off the central stem and wash them carefully. If the leaves are large, tear off the stems which will be correspondingly long. Tear very large leaves into manageable pieces. Large stems will require longer cooking than the leaves. Bok choy has Yin energy and so is stir-fried with ginger and garlic either on its own or with meat. It is also added to soup. (See Stir-fried greens with garlic, p. 154, Noodle soup, p. 97).

CHINESE CABBAGE, PEKING CABBAGE, NAPA CABBAGE, CELERY CABBAGE This cabbage is extremely versatile and is used in stir-fries and soups. In northern China it is often mixed with pork and used as a stuffing for dumplings. It readily absorbs flavors and provides an interesting texture. Chinese cabbages are available in many supermarkets. Some are long and cylindrical, others short and fat. All have tightly packed pale yellow or yellowy-green crinkled leaves. They are crisp with a sweet and delicate flavor. Avoid cabbages with tiny black spots – these are not fresh. Chinese cabbage will keep well for 2–3 weeks in the refrigerator.

To cook Pull off as many leaves as you need, wash them carefully, and stack them neatly on top of each other. Slice them as required with a heavy knife or cleaver. If the leaves seem slightly limp, you can crisp them up by soaking them for 30 minutes in cold salted water. This cabbage is not usually cooked as a single vegetable as its flavor is rather bland. (See Vegetable cake, p. 119.)

SPINACH There are two types of spinach grown in China: one is grown in water, the other in earth. Chinese water spinach has a hollow stem. It is a lighter green than the more familiar dark spinach and its leaves are smaller and more pointed. It is not recommended as a healthy vegetable for very active people as it causes the muscles to contract. It is usually cooked with plenty of garlic. If you are lucky enough to have a traditional cool and dry food storage area, you may find that spinach will survive reasonably well on the floor. In a refrigerator, it will quickly rot (see Storage, pp. 68–9).

To cook Wash well and shake dry. Spinach is good stir-fried on its own (see Stir-fried spinach, p. 134).

Clockwise from top left: bok choy, Chinese cabbage, long beans, water spinach, Chinese broccoli, sweet potato, Shanghai bok choy.

BEANS, LONG BEANS Either pale or dark green, these beans can grow up to 3 ft. long. They are very thin and often sold curled up and tied in bundles.

To cook Wash and cut into 2–3 inch lengths. Because they are so slender, the beans cook rapidly. You can stir-fry them with fermented bean curd or meat.

SWEET POTATO This is an edible tuber, like the ordinary potato. Because it is easy to grow even in poor, dry soil and stores well, it has become a popular staple crop in Asia. The tubers can be round or sausage-shaped, and the skin white, red, or purple. The flesh can be white or yellow. The varieties with yellow flesh are a good source of vitamin A and are often candied as a sweet for children. Look for smooth firm flesh. Store in a cool dry place. (See Sweet potato soup, p. 125.)

CHINESE BROCCOLI This is related to purple sprouting broccoli rather than regular broccoli. It has dark olive green leaves and white flowers, and a bitter, earthy taste. It will keep in the refrigerator for about three days.

To cook Break the shoots into 3 in. lengths. If you are using broccoli as an alternative, cut the large flower head into small flowerets about 1½ in. across. You can peel the skin and woody outer fibers of the thick stem and cut it into ¼ in. discs. Drop the broccoli pieces into lightly salted boiling water with a couple of drops of oil. Remove the broccoli after a few seconds and allow it to drain and cool before stir-frying. This blanching process will clean the broccoli and also fix the bright color.

STIR-FRIED BROCCOLI

¾ lb. broccoli
4 cloves garlic
¼ in. ginger root
1 tablespoon oil

Prepare the broccoli as described on the left. With the flat side of a cleaver or heavy knife tap each garlic clove and remove its skin. Cut the ginger into thin slices, then stack and shred them. Heat the wok, add the tablespoon of oil, and swirl it over the surface. Add the garlic cloves and shredded ginger and stir-fry for 1 minute to release the flavors. Now add the blanched broccoli and stir-fry for 3 minutes. Season with a few drops of oyster sauce or a pinch of salt. Transfer to a heated plate and serve.

Broccoli is usually stir-fried, either on its own or with dried mushrooms or meat. Occasionally you may find bunches of tiny mushrooms with tiny caps and 4 in. long, slender stems in Chinese stores. These are called golden mushrooms and are a great delicacy. They can also be stir-fried with broccoli.

EGGPLANT Native to tropical Asia, the eggplant can be shaped like an egg (hence the name), or like a long thin sausage. It ranges in color from white to purple. Chinese varieties are long and thin. These are less bitter than the short, plump types commonly available, and do not need salting to remove this taste before use. (See Eggplant with black bean sauce, p. 143.)

GREEN PEPPER This plant is grown worldwide. Peppers are very high in vitamin C. They reduce dampness, or excess fluid in the body tissue. Peppers are excellent in stir-fries (see Pork with green pepper and onion, p. 122).

SNOW PEAS These are smaller than sugar peas and much plumper but just as sweet. They stay crisper when cooked and will keep in the refrigerator for 4 to 5 days.

To cook Wash and cut off the tips, pulling off the stringy thread along the back as you do so. They are delicious as a single vegetable stir-fried with garlic or ginger. They are also good stir-fried with shrimp or meat.

You only need to cook them for 2 to 3 minutes. If you are cooking them with meat, cook the meat first and then remove it. Add the snow peas, garlic and ginger, stir-fry for 2 minutes, return the meat and stir-fry for 1 minute more.

WATER CHESTNUTS Although water chestnuts are popular, they do carry a health risk. The fresh ones in particular may be dangerous for some women during the early months of pregnancy, and it is unwise to eat them during menstruation.

Water chestnuts are the bulbs of a reed grown in paddy fields. Fresh ones often have mud on their reddish brown skin. Washed, peeled, and eaten raw, they are crisp and slightly sweet. Canned, they are not as wonderfully crisp. If fresh, they are best eaten on the day of purchase.

To cook They are sometimes cooked with lamb as they neutralize the strong smell of the meat. If canned, drain then rinse in cold water before using. They can be used in stir-fries with vegetables or meat to provide a different, crunchy texture. Any surplus will keep, covered with water, in the refrigerator for up to a week.

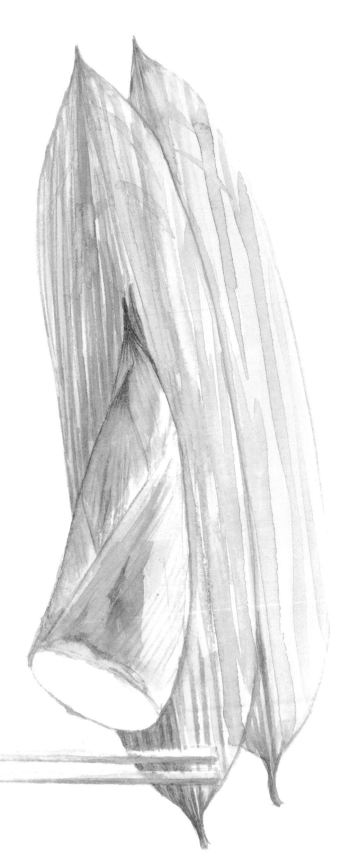

BAMBOO All over China and the Far East the bamboo plant is put to multiple use. The stems are used for scaffolding, for making furniture, cooking containers, water ladles, smoking pipes, and coat hangers. The ridged stem is used as a measure, and is split and woven into mats, hats, and containers of every shape and size. The leaves are used as a roofing material. In the kitchen, the bamboo plant rivals the soybean in its usefulness. The stems are used to make chopsticks, steamers, and baskets. The dried leaves are used to wrap delicious steamed parcels of rice and meat (see Jown, pp. 138–9). The young shoots are enjoyed by both pandas and humans.

FRESH BAMBOO SHOOTS are only seasonally available and can sometimes be found in Chinese or other Asian stores. Only the creamy yellow, tender central core of the stem is used. It is cut into sections and boiled for 5 minutes to remove the bitter taste, then sliced before being cooked.

Bamboo shoots have a lovely crunchy texture and slightly sweet flavor; they are used in soups and stir-fries. Canned bamboo shoots are available in chunks or slices. Any surplus will keep in a water-filled container for about 2 weeks in the refrigerator. Change the water every two days.

To cook Drain the bamboo shoots and rinse well. Blanch for 2 minutes in boiling water before using in your recipe. (See Hot and sour soup, p. 150.)

MEAT

Few animals are considered unsuitable to eat in China. Oxen were treated as a rare exception because the ox was considered too important a member of the family, devoting its days to hard labor in the fields. Every part of an ox, from its horns to its hooves, was used for some purpose. Its horns might be used as drinking vessels, its hooves to make buttons, its bones boiled first to make stock, then removed and fashioned into small tools or combs.

Nowadays, in places where the luxury of ox meat is easily available, many dishes include it. But the tradition of not wasting any part of an animal is preserved. For example, the feet of chicken or ducks are gently braised in a garlic broth until the skin and flesh can be sucked off the tiny bones. The belly cut of pork may be roasted, barbecued, or marinated and ground for stuffings. Its layers of fat, equally balanced with layers of lean muscle, keep it tender and sweet, thus transforming a cheap cut of meat into a delicious treat.

Shopping for meat takes place every day. The wise cook looks to see what has just arrived at the butcher's, or the market. The discerning eye seeks out the best quality and cuts. Except on special occasions, a large piece of meat will not be the main item in a Chinese meal. Small quantities of cheap cuts will be artfully combined with vegetables and light flavorings, accompanied by rice or noodles. The rice or noodles will constitute the bulk of a meal, with an average portion of 4 oz. for each person.

CHICKEN Chicken is highly prized in China. Each bird is sold live so that it can be inspected for health and age. Braised chicken feet are considered a great delicacy, and chicken blood may be added to soups or stir-fries. "White cooked" (poached) whole chicken will be served, delicately flavored with ginger, artfully cut into bite-sized pieces and then rearranged in the bird's natural shape. Chicken is normally cooked on the bone so that it doesn't shrink and dry out, having first been chopped into manageable pieces. The wings may be deep-fried until crisp, then sprinkled with a mixture of salt and Szechuan peppercorns. For those unable to inspect a live bird, a free-range chicken is recommended. It is bound to be healthier and tastier. (See chicken recipes on pp. 120, 130, 133.)

DUCK In China, duck sellers travel around with large crates of live ducks strapped to their bicycles. For the preparation of the famous Peking Duck, a slit is made in the neck and the skin inflated like a balloon. The duck is then marinated and hung up in a windy place to dry. This process separates the skin from the flesh and allows the thick layer of fat under the skin to melt more easily during cooking. Traditionally, Peking Duck was served as three courses. First came the crisp and tasty skin, served with mandarin pancakes, scallions, and plum sauce. Later in the meal, the braised, tenderized flesh featured as a delicacy. Later still a soup made from the bones would be served.

PORK This is the most popular meat in Chinese cuisine. In a Chinese supermarket the meat counter will have a good choice of different cuts. Pork belly is often stewed or braised and ground for stuffings. Spare-rib cuts will be used for the ever popular char siu (see below). Ground pork can be added to congee (see p. 128), giving a savory flavor and valuable protein. Fat cuts work well in longer-cooked, sweetish dishes like barbecued spare ribs. Ground fat cuts mixed with minced shrimp are often steamed.

CHAR SIU This Cantonese barbecued pork is difficult to make at home, and in Chinese communities there will be specialist suppliers of this sweet and subtly flavored meat. You may be able to buy it in Chinatown in shops which specialize in smoked and barbecued meats. It is used in small quantities in noodle dishes and soups (see Rice noodles, Singapore style, p. 149, Hot and sour soup, p. 150).

If you cannot buy char siu then use a well-flavored ham or leftover barbecued pork as a substitute.

CHINESE SAUSAGES You find wind-dried sausages in Chinese markets, hanging in pairs on strings, looking like plump, speckled wishbones. They are also sold vacuum packed. The sausages are about 6 in. long. The red/pink ones are made from pork meat, the darker brown ones from pork meat and duck liver. They have a sweet flavor, sugar balancing the salt, both of them acting as preservatives. The sausages can be steamed whole, then cut into slices, or sliced and added to stir-fries and other dishes (see Chicken, Chinese mushroom and sausage casserole, p. 95, Vegetable cake, p. 119).

LAMB AND GOAT Lamb and goat tend to be eaten only in the colder northern areas of China. The flesh of these thick-coated animals is slowly cooked to provide protein-rich meals that warm and soothe the stomach. As with pork, the belly cut of lamb is popular and would be the preferred cut for the winter recipe, Stewed bean curd with lamb, p. 152.

BEEF The grainy texture of beef makes a wonderful contrast to slippery noodles, and its flavor is nicely complimented by soy and oyster sauce. Because beef is a larger animal, the muscles are long, making it even more important to slice across the grain as thinly as possible so that the meat will be cooked and tenderized in a very short time (see Ginger and pineapple beef, p. 132).

FISH AND SHELLFISH

Sea and freshwater fish are abundant along China's long coastline and throughout its extensive river systems. The country offers an extraordinary variety of delicious fish and seafood recipes. Restaurants, hotels, and banqueting halls offer steamed fish drizzled with seasoned hot oil, fresh lobster – cooked, cut into pieces, and reassembled into its natural shape – and other delicacies such as steamed eel delicately flavored with ginger. The adventurous eater does not have to look far to find establishments featuring endless exotic sea animals and vegetables.

Even the freshest of fish can be spoiled by overcooking. The Chinese techniques of gentle steaming and quick stir-frying offer the perfect solution. Freshly caught fish are always steamed so that the subtle flavor can be savored. Small, delicate fish will not be damaged by steaming. Larger fish with firm flesh, such as cod, can be cut into chunks, marinated, and quickly stir-fried without disintegrating. Strongly flavored oily fish are often steamed in black bean sauce or stir-fried and served with another tasty sauce to balance the powerful fish flavor. Frozen fish or fish that are not fresh are usually cooked and served in this way.

In China, no part of a fish is wasted. If the flesh is to be stir-fried, the head and bones may be used to make stock for a fish soup.

SHELLFISH The humble shrimp enjoys widespread popularity throughout the Chinese world and is ideal for fast cooking. Shelled and deveined, it is used in soups, stir-fries, and steamed dishes. Frozen shrimp are not regarded as a good substitute for fresh ones. However, they are much easier to find and are already prepared. Minced shrimp is often used as a filling for the ever popular dim sum.

ELEGANT DINING

Whatever the meat or fish, if it is to be presented whole at the meal table, there will never be any need for a carving knife and fork. It is considered a sign of barbarism to have a knife at the table. The whole bird or fish will have been fully prepared in the kitchen, carefully cut into small pieces before being artfully reassembled into its natural shape.

THE *Four*

SEASONS

THE FOUR SEASONS

The four seasons are the rhythm of Yin and Yang. This continual flux is represented by the five circles on the facing page.

In the central circle, the power of Yin is represented by the dark curve on top. The force of Yang is symbolized by the light curve underneath. At the broadest end of the dark curve, where Yin is at its greatest, is Winter.

If you follow the line of the outer circle around to the left, you immediately come to the thinnest end of the light curve. This is the beginning of Yang, the emergence of Spring.

As the Yang curve expands upward, it reaches its fullest power. This is Summer.

At the point where Yang is at its fullest, the dark curve of Yin begins. This is the starting point of Autumn.

As with all symbols, the reality it represents is more subtle than the two-dimensional drawing itself. Instinctively we know that Spring is already present in Winter long before we see the first shoots pushing up through the snow. We can feel the presence of Autumn while all around us we see only Summer. This truth is represented schematically by the little white circle of Yang drawn inside the darkness of Yin and by the dark circle of Yin which you find inside the fullness of Yang.

The interaction of Yin and Yang is organic, not linear. Each gives birth to the other. While they are as opposite as night and day, each emerges out of the power of the other. Long before either Yin or Yang emerge, each is present, invisibly growing within its apparent opposite. Understood in this way, Spring and Autumn are the transitions between the Yin of Winter and the Yang of Summer.

The transition from Yin to Yang is a matter of great significance. It is the interface between the two halves of light and dark. This curve is the energy of Earth, the ever present, nurturing force out of which all life emerges and to which all life returns.

The other four energies – Fire, Metal, Water, and Wood – are also present. Summer is the season of upward moving Fire energy. The condensing energy of Metal is manifested in Autumn. Water energy, which descends, is predominant in Winter. The expansive energy of Wood is expressed in Spring.

Earth energy is present throughout the cycle, as a stabilizing force, particularly evident in the latter part of each season when the transformation of energy into a new pattern takes place.

The four circles that surround the central symbol hold the key to eating in accordance with the seasons. They are explained in the four introductions to the seasonal recipes.

Each seasonal section gives you a sample breakfast, a soup, a selection of main courses, and a suggested dessert. You may choose only one dish for a meal or you may make a selection for a three-course lunch or dinner. You may substitute ingredients. Don't feel you are restricted to the recipes you are given in these pages. You may add a seasonal dish to your cooking whenever you feel like it.

SUMMER

AUTUMN

SPRING

WINTER

SPRING RECIPES

As the fullness of Yin changes into Yang, there is a period of transition. This is Spring, the transition of the natural world from Winter to Summer. "In Spring," says the physician of the Yellow Emperor, "the pulse of the stomach should be fine and delicate like the strings of a musical instrument. Then it will be healthy and well-balanced." He warns: "The illnesses caused by Wind in Spring will affect the digestion in Summer."

Spring is the season of growth. The natural world begins to open itself outward. It is the season of expansion.

We feel the changes in our own bodies. The sluggishness of Winter is past. We are leaving behind the months of cold and penetrating damp. Our energy is rekindled.

The small circle to the lower left of the large Yin/Yang tells us what we need in this time of transition. For balance in Winter, the season of maximum Yin, we will have needed a diet with a preponderance of Yang energy. Now in Spring, we are heading toward Summer when Yang energy will be at its height. Our diet will change to one in which Yin foods predominate. The Spring months should be the time in which we carefully ease ourselves through this transformation. Our diet should be equally balanced between Yin and Yang. Thus the little circle is equally divided between light and dark.

The accumulated energy we stored throughout the winter months is released in Spring. The body no longer needs the fat it has used to protect itself against the cold. Spring is not the season for fatty foods and grease. It is a time for inner cleaning. It is time for soups that help to clear the inner organs and loosen the joints.

The recipes in this section have been selected as sample seasonal dishes that will help your body leave the Winter months behind and prepare itself for the energy of Summer.

ALL RECIPES SERVE 4 PEOPLE

Dim Sum 116

Steamed Pork Dumplings 116–17

Scallion Pancakes 118

Vegetable Cake 119

Chicken and Corn Soup 120

Pork with Green Pepper and Onion 122

Steamed Fish
with Ginger and Scallion 123

Tomato with Beef and Eggs 124

Sweet Potato Soup 125

DIM SUM

These wonderful filled steamed dumplings can be eaten any time of day, any season. In Hong Kong many restaurants only serve dim sum with an amazing variety of fillings. They have never been a part of home cooking, as they require such specialized skills. Chefs are trained specifically for this task. In Chinese supermarkets look in the freezer section for packs of dim sum with mixed fillings. Allow 4–6 dumplings per person.

How to steam prepared frozen dim sum

If you would like dim sum for breakfast, take them out of the freezer and defrost overnight in the refrigerator. For an afternoon snack, put them on a plate and defrost at room temperature for 1 hour.

To steam dim sum, set up your steamer – a stacking bamboo steamer (see p. 86) is ideal. Place a cabbage leaf inside each layer and arrange the dumplings on top with plenty of space between them. (The cabbage leaf will prevent the dumplings from sticking to the steamer.)

When the water in the wok is boiling, stack the steamers in it, cover and steam for about 12 minutes. To test the dumplings, insert a metal skewer into the thickest part, if it comes out clean the dumplings are cooked.

Dim sum are normally brought to the table in a bamboo steamer which rests on a plate.

STEAMED PORK DUMPLINGS

These dumplings are quite easy to make at home. They can be steamed or fried (see variation opposite). You can serve them with dipping sauces of red rice vinegar or chili oil (see opposite). The amount of water needed to make the dough will depend on the absorbency of the flour you use, so the quantity given here is a rough guide. The amounts given will make 48–56 dumplings.

for the dough:
2½ cups unbleached all-purpose flour
about ¾ cup cold water

for the filling:
½ lb. pork, not too lean
1 lb. Chinese cabbage
7 scallions
2 teaspoons salt

marinade for the pork:
½ teaspoon salt
½ teaspoon sugar
2 teaspoons light soy sauce
2 teaspoons oil
1 teaspoon cornstarch mixed with
1 tablespoon water

First prepare the dough. Put the flour into a large bowl and very slowly add the water, stirring until the flour forms strips which stick together to form a rough ball shape; it should be moist but not too sticky. Place the ball of dough on a floured board and knead it until it is smooth and elastic. Cover it with a clean damp cloth and leave to stand for 1 hour.

Now prepare the filling. Break the leaves off the cabbage and wash them carefully. Drain and stack them in a pile. With a large knife or cleaver cut them into very fine shreds, then chop roughly. Put them in a bowl, sprinkle with the salt, and let them stand for 20 minutes.

Finely chop the pork with a cleaver or mince in a food processor, put it in a bowl and add the marinade ingredients. Stir well.

Wash the scallions, trim off the roots. Slice both the green and white parts finely.

Tip the cabbage into a strainer and squeeze off the excess moisture. Put it into a bowl with the pork and scallions. Mix well.

Now you are ready to make the dumplings. Take the dough ball and cut it into four equal pieces. Using the palms of both hands, roll each piece of dough into a long sausage shape, then cut into 12–14 pieces. Quickly roll each small lump between the palms of your hands into a little ball, then, using a floured rolling pin, roll each ball into a circle measuring about 3 in. across.

Now put a circle of dough in the palm of one hand and with a spoon put about 1½ teaspoons of filling in the center. Close your hand slightly and with the other hand pinch the edges of the dough together. Now crinkle the sealed edge by squeezing it at intervals, first one way then the other; this will both tighten the seal and make the dumplings look more attractive.

The dumplings may need to be cooked in three batches, in a 3-tiered bamboo steamer with 5–6 dumplings per layer. They take only 8–10 minutes to steam, then transfer to a heated plate and serve.

Dips
Red rice vinegar is a lovely pink color and has a mild, sweetish flavor. Simply pour about 3 tablespoons into a small bowl or saucer. The dumplings are also good dipped in chili oil. This is easy to find in Chinese or other Asian supermarkets.

VARIATION

You can also cook the dumplings in another most interesting way, boiled and fried. You need a large, heavy-bottomed frying pan with a lid. Heat the frying pan and add 2 tablespoons of oil, swirl it around to cover the whole surface. Now fill the base of the pan with the dumplings just touching each other. Put on the lid and cook for 3 minutes. Lower the heat and add about ½ in. of hot water, replace the lid and cook over high heat for about 8 minutes. The dumplings should be golden brown on the bottom and the water should have been absorbed. Remove to a heated plate and serve.

SCALLION PANCAKES

This may seem a long-winded recipe, but it is quite simple and fast to prepare, and preparing dough is good exercise in the morning. The cake is an excellent accompaniment to congee, and is best eaten immediately.

As the absorbency of flour is unpredictable it is hard to give an exact quantity of water needed to form the dough. The suggested quantities given here are for four people.

2½ cups unbleached all-purpose flour
1 cup very hot water
8 scallions, finely chopped
1 teaspoon salt
oil for shallow frying

You will need a medium-sized, heatproof bowl, a floured board or clean surface, and a rolling pin.

Put the flour into the bowl, add a little of the hot water and stir vigorously. The flour will start to form small lumps. Continue until it forms one large soft lump; it should not be sticky.

VARIATION

If you would like a richer taste you can add ground fat from pork belly before adding the scallion.

Remove the dough to a floured board and knead it rhythmically until it is very smooth and elastic (about 5 minutes). Put it back into the bowl and cover with a damp cloth. (This will prevent the surface of the dough from becoming hard and dry.) Leave it to rest for half an hour.

Divide the dough into four, take one piece and roll it into a ball between the palms of your hands. Now using a rolling pin, roll it into a circle about ⅛ in. thick.

Brush the surface of the dough with oil to within ½ in. of the edges. Sprinkle it evenly with a little salt and some chopped scallion.

Now carefully roll up the dough into a long sausage and coil it around itself, like a snake. Repeat this process and put the second snake on top of the first. Now flatten by lightly rolling with rolling pin, or just using your hands, so that the cake is about ½ in. thick.

Repeat this process with the two remaining lumps of dough to make a second cake.

Heat the wok and add ¼ in. of oil. Add a cake and over medium heat fry one side until golden, turn and fry the other side. Remove with a slotted spoon and drain on a paper towel. Slice the cake and serve while piping hot and crisp. The first cake will probably have been eaten before you finish cooking the second one.

VEGETABLE CAKE

This most unusual cake is a kind of steamed savory pudding – light, nourishing, and easy to digest. Non-vegetarians may like to add dried shrimp and Chinese sausage.

This recipe makes a large quantity so you will need to use a big shallow heatproof dish in a large steamer. Otherwise, you could use two shallow 1 lb. loaf pans or tinfoil containers, side by side in a large steamer.

3–4 dried Chinese mushrooms
¼ cup dried shrimp (optional)
1 quart water
1 lb. Chinese cabbage
4 teaspoons salt
1 Chinese sausage (optional)
1–2 scallions, green parts only
1 tablespoon oil
1 tablespoon sugar
1 tablespoon salt
2 tablespoons dark soy sauce
¼ teaspoon white pepper
few drops sesame oil
2 cups rice flour

Put the mushrooms and shrimp into a bowl with ¾ cup of water and leave to soak, preferably overnight.

Take the leaves off the cabbage and wash them carefully, then stack them into a pile and slice them finely across into strips.

Bring 3 cups of water to boil in a pan, add the cabbage and 1 teaspoon salt, cover, and cook over a low heat for 5 minutes. Remove from the heat and set aside. Do not drain as you will be using the water later.

Lift the mushrooms and shrimp from their bowl and keep the soaking water. Discard the woody stems of the mushrooms and slice the tops thinly.

Slice the Chinese sausage thinly. Chop the scallions finely.

Heat the wok, add 1 tablespoon of oil, and swirl over the surface. Add the sausage and stir-fry, add the shrimp and mushrooms and stir-fry until they release their fragrance, then remove from the heat.

Add the mushroom and shrimp water to the pot with the cabbage and its water. Add the sausage, mushrooms and shrimp, the sugar, salt, dark soy sauce, white pepper, and a few drops of sesame oil.

Leave to stand for a moment, then slowly sprinkle the rice flour on top and, with a pair of chopsticks, stir constantly until all the flour has been absorbed and the liquid is white and thick. Stir in the scallions.

Pour the mixture into a large, oiled, shallow dish or pan, cover the top with wax paper or aluminum foil and steam for 1 hour (see p. 86). Test with a chopstick, if it comes out clean the cake is cooked. Transfer the cake to a plate, or cut into sections and serve from the dish or pan.

This recipe goes well with scallion pancakes, noodles, or congee. You can store it for 2–3 days in the refrigerator. To reheat, remove the sections and gently fry both sides, serve with hoisin or chili sauce.

CHICKEN AND CORN SOUP

This is a splendid example of how the Chinese incorporate American ingredients to create a very delicate and delicious Chinese-style dish. Its creamy flavor is especially popular with children. The soup is quick to make with canned creamed corn. Otherwise, you may chop whole corn kernels, or use fresh, frozen or canned corn instead.

1 skinned and boned chicken breast

for the marinade:
pinch of salt
1 teaspoon light soy sauce
1 teaspoon cornstarch dissolved in
1 tablespoon water

1–1¼ cups corn
1 small egg
1 quart water
1 teaspoon salt
a little white pepper

VARIATION

You can try this recipe using crabmeat, shrimp or sliced fish instead of chicken. If you are vegetarian, you may substitute tofu. You may also thicken the soup to your taste by adding a little cornstarch mixed with cold water before you add the egg.

Chop the chicken finely. Put it into a bowl, add the marinade ingredients, stir carefully and allow to steep while you prepare the other ingredients.

If you are using whole kernels, fresh, frozen, or canned, chop them roughly. You can do this by hand or in a food processor. (You will need to defrost frozen kernels before chopping.)

In a small bowl beat the egg with a little salt.

Boil 1 quart water in a pan, add the corn and 1 teaspoon salt and bring it back to a boil.

Now add the marinated chicken, bring back to a boil for at least two minutes and stir well to break up the meat. Cook for at least two minutes until all the chicken has turned white. Turn off the heat and, using chopsticks, stir in a circular motion as you slowly drizzle in the egg, so that it cooks in long strands.

Remove the pan from the heat, allow to stand for a moment then transfer to a heated bowl, sprinkle with a little white pepper and serve.

Top left, Scallion pancakes; top right, Steamed fish with ginger and scallion; bottom right, Vegetable cake; bottom left, Pork with green pepper and onion; center, Sweet potato soup.

THE
FOUR
SEASONS
ame ``.

THE
FOUR
SEASONS

PORK WITH GREEN PEPPER AND ONION

This recipe is most suited to Spring, when our bodies need to become lighter. All through the Winter we have been less active and probably accumulated excess water. Here, the green pepper and onion have a mild diuretic effect. We are using pork, but you could substitute chicken, beef, shrimp, or fish. If you wish you could add a little sliced chili with the black beans and garlic.

1½ lb. boned shoulder, leg, or tenderloin of pork

for the marinade:
2 teaspoons light soy sauce
½ teaspoon sugar
a pinch of salt
1 teaspoon cornstarch dissolved in
1 tablespoon water
a few drops of oil

2½ tablespoons oil
1 medium-sized green pepper
3 tablespoons water
1 fresh red chili, sliced
1 medium-sized onion
½ tablespoon fermented black beans
(25–30 beans)
5–6 cloves of garlic

Using a cleaver or sharp knife, slice the pork as thinly as possible. This is easier to do if the meat is semifrozen. (Place the meat in the freezer for half an hour before slicing.) Put the sliced meat into a bowl, add the marinade, stir well and set aside.

Cut the pepper in half through the stem, remove the stem, pith, and seeds and wash the flesh. Cut each half into two; continue cutting each piece in half until you have 1 in. square pieces.

Cut the onion in half through the root, trim off the root from each half, and pull the skin off. Cut each half into 3 lengthwise and cut each piece in half.

Heat the wok; add 1½ tablespoons of the oil, and swirl it around to cover the whole surface. Over high heat add the pork and stir-fry for 2–3 minutes. With a slotted spoon, remove the pork and transfer to a plate.

Add 1 tablespoon of oil to the wok, lower the heat, and add the black beans, sliced chili and garlic. Stir-fry for a moment then add the green pepper, the onion, and 3 tablespoons water. Cover and cook for a maximum of 4 minutes. If you cook for longer than this the green pepper and onion will become soggy and the dish will be spoiled.

Now add the pork; stir and cook for a further 2 minutes. Remove to a heated plate and serve.

STEAMED FISH WITH GINGER AND SCALLION

For this recipe you can use a small whole fish such as herring or sea bass or fillets of a larger fish such as cod. It depends on the size of steamer you have available (see p. 86). Never add salt or soy sauce before cooking as this will toughen the flesh. Soy sauce added before cooking will also mask the taste of a delicately flavored fish too much. However, if you would like to mask the flavor of a strong tasting fish, you can spread some crushed black beans and garlic on top before steaming.

1½ lb. fish
2 scallions
1 in. fresh ginger root
a little oil
1 tablespoon light soy sauce

Prepare the fish or, if it has been gutted by the fish seller, wash it carefully inside and out and pat dry with paper towels.

Wash the scallions and trim off the roots; cut off the white parts then cut the green parts into 1½ in. lengths.

Slice the ginger into ⅛ in.-thick pieces across the grain. There is no need to peel it. Put the green parts of the scallion and 1 ginger slice aside.

Select an oval plate to suit the size of fish and lay the white scallion pieces side by side with the ginger slices between them. Arrange the fish on top; the scallion and ginger flavors will gently permeate the fish during steaming and also prevent the fish from sticking to the plate. You can remove the scallion and ginger after steaming if you wish, or transfer the fish to a heated plate.

Prepare the steamer (see p. 86) and when it is ready, cook the fish for 8–10 minutes depending on thickness. If you like your fish to be very well done you can test by inserting a chopstick into the thickest part and it should go right through. Do not overcook.

Take the remaining slice of ginger and shred it finely. When the fish is almost ready, heat a wok and add a little oil, the green scallion and the shredded slice of ginger. Stir-fry briefly.

Remove the fish from the steamer.

Add 1 tablespoon light soy sauce to the ginger and scallion in the wok and stir; immediately pour the hot garnish over the fish to sear the skin and add flavor.

TOMATO WITH BEEF AND EGGS

This recipe will tempt even tomato haters to eat this fruit, which is very high in vitamin C. With the eggs, beef and the tart flavor of the tomatoes softened by the addition of sugar, the flavor of this dish is rich but subtle.

¼ lb. beef steak

for the marinade:
I teaspoon light soy sauce
a pinch of salt
I teaspoon sugar
I teaspoon cornstarch dissolved in
I tablespoon of cold water
a few drops of oil

I lb. tomatoes
4 eggs
½ teaspoon salt
2 tablespoons oil
⅓ cup water
up to 3 tablespoons sugar (depending on sweetness of tomatoes)

Chop the beef finely, or mince roughly in a food processor if you prefer. Put it into a bowl, add the marinade ingredients and stir well.

Wash the tomatoes and chop them into quarters. It is healthier to leave the skins on.

Beat the eggs with ½ teaspoon salt until the yolks and whites are combined.

Heat the wok, add 1 tablespoon oil, and swirl it around to cover the whole surface of the pan. Add the eggs; stir-fry them quickly until they are set, then remove to a plate.

Add 1 tablespoon of oil to the wok and then the tomatoes with ⅓ cup water and sugar to taste. Stir-fry, then leave to cook over medium heat for 5 minutes or until the tomatoes are soft and mushy.

Add the beef and stir-fry for 1 minute or until all the meat has changed color. Now add the eggs, mix well and serve.

VARIATION

If you find the taste of this dish too rich, or you don't like beef, then try this recipe omitting the beef. If you do this you can add a little salt to taste.

SWEET POTATO SOUP

Sweet potatoes are readily available in large supermarkets as well as specialty stores. There are two easily obtainable varieties of sweet potato (see p. 104). For this recipe choose the orange-fleshed type. This is a sweet soup, with an extremely unusual and interesting taste. It is guaranteed to stimulate the palate.

The recipe uses sliced sugar (see p. 92) which is available in Chinese or Asian grocery stores and has its own special taste. The ginger adds a piquant flavor to the sweet potato.

As a rule of thumb, once the stick of sugar is dissolved, the soup is ready.

1 lb. sweet potato
6 in. piece (3 oz.) fresh ginger root
two 5 in. x 1 in. x ½ in. pieces of
sliced sugar (around 5 oz.)
2½ cups water

Peel the sweet potato and cut it into 1 in. cubes or ¼ in. thick slices.

Clean the ginger and cut it across the grain into ⅛ in. thick slices. There is no need to peel it.

In a pot, boil 2½ cups water, add the ginger slices, and cook for 4 minutes.

Remove the ginger slices and add the sweet potato. Boil for 3 minutes. Add the sugar, and continue to boil until the sugar has melted and the sweet potato is cooked. Transfer to a heated bowl and serve.

When Yin has been completely transformed into Yang, there is a season of fullness. This is Summer. "In Summer," says the physician of the Yellow Emperor, "the pulse of the stomach should be like the beating of a hammer. Then it will be healthy and well-balanced." He warns: "The illnesses caused by the heat of Summer will result in Autumn fevers."

Summer is the season of maturity. The natural world expresses its full power. It is the season of intensity.

The small circle to the upper left of the large Yin/Yang tells us what we need in this time of transition. For balance in Spring, the transition between maximum Yin and Yang, we need a diet equally balanced between the two. Now in Summer, Yang energy will be at its height. Our diet will need to change to one in which Yin foods predominate. The Summer months should be the time in which we take care not to overheat. Our diet should be the counterbalance to the intensity of Yang. Thus the little circle shows a greater expanse of dark and a smaller proportion of light.

Our bodies heat up in Summer and we respond by sweating. We need to replenish our inner reserves of liquid and salts. This is the season for the water stored in vegetables and fruits. There will be many more of these in our diet. The salt content in our cooking will increase as well. It is also the season when we naturally drink more of all fluids. But there is a warning here: chilled drinks have a charming effect in the mouth, but inside the body, they play havoc with our mechanisms for heat control. Instead of helping the body release unwanted heat, they reverse the process.

In the heat of Summer, our digestion becomes lazy. We are surrounded by the intoxicating energy of the season and we feel less need for food. We tend to fill ourselves with fluids and pay less attention to substantial meals. We need to stimulate our appetites. These are good months for eating a few smaller meals each day. This is the ideal time for sweet and sour dishes and the tempting aromas and flavors of other spicy foods.

The recipes in this section have been selected as sample seasonal dishes that will help your body emerge from the transition of Spring into the full splendor of Summer.

ALL RECIPES SERVE 4 PEOPLE

SOYBEAN SOUP AND DOUGH STICKS

All over China freshly made soy milk is available. Warming and nourishing, it is often heated and drunk as a soup for breakfast. If you cannot find fresh soy milk, you can make up your own easily from packets of tofu mix or soybean curd mix. Simply follow the instructions on the pack for the quantity of water to be added, but do not add the small pack of coagulant – the mix will set into tofu.

You could also use heat-treated soy milk, which will have its own particular flavor. It is a good idea to sample different milks to find the taste you like.

In China, soybean soup is traditionally eaten with "ghost," also called dough sticks. These are crunchy sticks of deep-fried dough, which you dip in the soup before eating. They are about 10 in. long and look like a couple of bones stuck together. Crisp on the outside, they are chewy on the inside, and can be bought in Chinese bakeries.

Dough sticks are difficult to make at home; they need special flour and also a large quantity of frying oil because they are so long. You could also try the soup with a croissant, brioche, or hot, crisp baguette.

For 4 people, make up 5 cups of the soybean powder, warm it gently in a pan, and sweeten to taste before serving in warm bowls.

CONGEE

This savory rice porridge dish may be eaten at any time of day and is often served with fried noodles. Fish, pork, chicken, or shredded lettuce may be added to make it more substantial. It is ideal for babies and invalids if you leave out the salt and oil.

3 quarts water
1 cup long grain, short grain, or
Japanese rice
½ teaspoon salt
a few drops of oil
¼ lb. pork

for the marinade:
½ teaspoon cornstarch dissolved in
½ tablespoon cold water
¼ teaspoon sugar
¼ teaspoon light soy sauce

In a large, lidded pot, bring 3 quarts water to a boil. Wash the rice quickly and tip it into the pot; add the salt and a few drops of oil. Bring back to the boil and stir to separate the rice grains. Put on the lid and boil for 1 hour. Check occasionally to make sure that the rice is not sticking to the pot.

Slice or mince the pork finely, add the marinade ingredients and stir well.

When the rice is cooked, add the pork; bring back to a boil, simmer for 5 minutes, then serve. If you are using chicken or fish you need only cook it for 2 minutes.

To speed the cooking time, soak the rice in a little water with the salt and oil for half an hour and then boil for 30–45 minutes.

BEANSPROUT NOODLES

If you like crisp beansprouts, try to buy them fresh rather than canned, or sprout your own from mung beans (see p. 99).

1 medium-sized onion
3½–4 cups beansprouts
3 scallions
1 lb. noodles
2 tablespoons oil
a little ground white pepper
a pinch of salt
1 teaspoon sugar
2 tablespoons light soy sauce
2 tablespoons oyster sauce

QUICK CONGEE RECIPE

You can save time by using leftover rice to make your congee, even more if you reduce the rice to a paste in a food processor or blender, adding a little water. Boil 2 cups of water and add the mashed rice, boil for 5 minutes. Add flavorings of your choice and simmer for 5 minutes.

Cut through the root of the onion and peel off the skin, cut it in half and then into thin slices.

Clean the beansprouts, discarding any that are brown.

Wash the scallions, trim off the roots and cut them into 1½ in. lengths.

Boil plenty of water in a large pot, add the noodles, and stir to separate them. Turn off the heat, cover, and leave to stand for a few minutes. To test whether they are cooked, lift a noodle; it should be soft and pliable, and, if you break it, the same color all through. Tip the noodles into a colander and plunge them into cold water or rinse them well under a cold tap and leave them to drain. This will stop them from cooking further and sticking together. You can cut them into 6 in. lengths to make them easier to handle.

Heat the wok, add 2 tablespoons oil, and swirl it around to cover the whole surface. Add the sliced onion and stir-fry, then add the noodles and stir-fry.

Now add the beansprouts and scallions and stir thoroughly. If you like your beansprouts soft, add them to the wok before the noodles. Sprinkle with a little white pepper, a pinch of salt, the sugar, and the soy sauce. Finally, add the oyster sauce and stir. Remove to a heated plate and serve.

CHINESE MUSHROOM AND CHICKEN SOUP

The mushrooms in this recipe help to lower blood pressure and break down stored body fat. However, it is advisable to eat this dish only once a week. You can omit the chicken and replace it with tofu and/or peas or carrots if you wish.

8 medium-sized dried Chinese mushrooms
2½ cups water
1 boned and skinned chicken breast

for the marinade:
½ teaspoon sugar
1 teaspoon light soy sauce
1 teaspoon cornstarch dissolved in
1 tablespoon cold water

a little salt
1 scallion

Clean the mushrooms and put them into a bowl with 1¼ cups of water. Leave them to soak, either overnight if you plan to use them in the morning, or in the morning if you will use them that evening.

Cut the chicken into ½ in. cubes, put them into a bowl and add the marinade ingredients, stir well.

Lift the mushrooms out of their water, but don't throw the water away as you will be using it in the soup. Remove any woody stems and slice the mushrooms thinly.

Wash the scallion and trim off the root. Chop it finely, both white and green parts.

Pour the remaining 1¼ cups of water into a pot and bring it to a boil. Add the mushroom water, taking care not to include any sediment which may have collected at the bottom. Bring it back to a boil.

Now add the sliced mushrooms and marinated chicken and simmer for 2 minutes. Be careful not to extend this cooking time. If the chicken is overcooked it will toughen and have a rough texture.

Remove the pot from the heat, add a little salt and sprinkle with the chopped scallion. Transfer to a heated bowl and serve.

Top left, Congee; top right, Ginger and pineapple beef; bottom right, Chinese mushroom and chicken soup; bottom left, Mushroom chicken; center, Dried bean curd with eggs.

GINGER AND PINEAPPLE BEEF

This fresh, fragrant dish is excellent during summer when you feel too hot and try to cool down by drinking lots of liquid. Your stomach feels bloated and you don't feel hungry when it is time to eat.

Look for pickled ginger in a Chinese supermarket. Make sure it is young ginger; the slices should be very thin, creamy in color and tinged with pink. You will be able to see that older ginger has a stringy texture.

1 lb. beef steak

for the marinade:
2 teaspoons light soy sauce
1 teaspoon sugar
1 teaspoon cornstarch dissolved in
1 tablespoon water
1 teaspoon oil

8 oz. can of pineapple rings
a heaped ½ cup of pickled ginger
1 scallion
1 tablespoon oil

It is important to cut the beef across the grain. You will see that the long muscle fibers all lie in one direction. Cut at right angles to them; the meat will be far more tender.

Cut the beef into thin slices, put it into a bowl, add the marinade ingredients, and stir.

Drain the juice from the pineapple and cut each of the rings into six pieces.

Lift out the slices of ginger until you have the required amount and set aside.

Wash the scallion and trim off the root. Chop it into 1 in. pieces.

Heat the wok, add the oil, and swirl it around to cover the whole surface. Add the beef and stir-fry for 1 minute.

Add the pineapple pieces and the sliced ginger and stir-fry for 2 minutes.

Add the scallion and quickly stir it in; transfer to a heated plate and serve.

VARIATION

This recipe is also delicious using leftover roast duck.

MUSHROOM CHICKEN

This dish has a pleasant straw color enlivened by the fresh bright green and white of the scallions.

1 lb. boned skinned chicken

for the marinade:
2 tablespoons light soy sauce
1 teaspoon sugar
1 teaspoon salt
1 teaspoon cornstarch mixed with
1 tablespoon water
a few drops of oil

1 small onion
1 lb. button mushrooms
2 scallions
2 tablespoons oil
½ teaspoon sugar
1 tablespoon oyster sauce

Slice the chicken thinly and put it into a bowl. Add the marinade ingredients and set aside.

Trim off the root of the onion and peel off the skin. Cut it in half lengthwise. Cut each half crossways into 3 pieces and then each piece in half.

Clean the mushrooms.

Wash the scallions and trim off the roots. Cut them into 1 in. lengths.

Heat the wok, add 2 tablespoons oil, and swirl it around to coat the surface. Add the chicken and the marinade and stir-fry for 2 minutes.

Add the onion and scallions and stir-fry for 1 minute.

Now add the sugar and the oyster sauce and stir.

Lastly, add the mushrooms and stir-fry for 30 seconds. Remove to a plate and serve.

VARIATION

Instead of the chicken you may use shrimp or beef for this recipe. You may also use pork, but you will need to stir-fry it for longer – about 4 minutes should be enough.

STIR-FRIED SPINACH

The fermented bean curd or "Chinese cheese" in this recipe adds a most interesting flavor. You can use Chinese or another variety of spinach for this dish (see p. 103). Use large spinach leaves rather than tiny young ones as they have more flavor. If you are nervous of chili just use half a pod the first time you make this recipe.

2 teaspoons salt
2 lb. spinach
2 small fresh red chilies
1 in. fresh ginger root
8 cloves garlic
3 tablespoons oil
3 cubes fermented bean curd
a little sugar to taste

Add 2 teaspoons salt to a large bowl of water and wash the spinach thoroughly. The salt will help to remove any earth and germs. Shake off the excess water. If the leaves are large, with long stems, trim off the stems and discard them.

Wash the chilies and slice them thinly across. Discard the green stems. Wash your knife, board, and hands before doing anything else. The oil from the chili can irritate skin and eyes.

Clean the ginger root and cut it into thin slices across the grain. Do not peel.

Using the broad side of a heavy knife or cleaver, tap each clove of garlic. You can now remove the skin very easily.

Heat the wok, add 3 tablespoons oil, and swirl it around to cover the whole surface.

Add the ginger slices and stir-fry them over a high heat until they release their fragrance. Add the garlic and quickly stir-fry.

Now add the cubes of fermented bean curd and the sliced chili. The bean curd will reduce to a mash as you stir-fry it with the other ingredients.

Now add the spinach and stir-fry briefly until the leaves are wilted and coated with the sauce. At this stage you can add a little sugar to balance the saltiness of the bean curd, if you like.

Remove to a heated plate and serve.

DRIED BEAN CURD WITH EGGS

This sweet soup is made from dried bean curd sheets (or bean curd skin). These sheets are literally the skin that forms on the top of the great steaming cauldrons of soybean liquid used to make tofu. This skin is lifted off and dried. It is very thin and softens quickly when cooked. Look for packets of dried bean curd sheets where the sheets are paper thin; they are so fragile that they may have already broken up into small fragments. If the sheets are not paper thin they will not dissolve. The thicker sheets are softened and rolled up to form a vegetarian-style "chicken".

The soup is sweetened with rock sugar (see p. 92), which imparts a lovely rich sticky flavor. If it is hard to find, use natural turbinado or granulated sugar instead.

1 quart water
four 8 in. x 12 in. dried bean curd
sheets (about 2 oz.)
2 eggs
5–6 oz. rock sugar

Pour the water into a pan and bring it to a boil.

Crush the bean curd sheets into small fragments while they are still in the pack. Add the crushed bean curd sheets to the boiling water, lower the heat to a slow simmer, and cook for 40–50 minutes, stirring occasionally.

When the bean curd has dissolved, bring the liquid to a boil and add the rock sugar.

After the sugar has dissolved reduce the heat to very low.

Break the eggs into a bowl and beat well. Slowly add the eggs to the pot, whisking all the while. They will form into silky strands floating in the rich sweet syrup.

Transfer to a heated bowl and serve.

This recipe is very nourishing and is recommended for pregnant women.

As the fullness of Yang changes into Yin, there is a period of transition. This is Autumn, when the natural world is transformed from Summer into Winter. "In Autumn," says the physician of the Yellow Emperor, "the pulse of the stomach should be small and rough. Then it will be healthy and well-balanced." He warns: "The dampness of Autumn causes coughing in Winter."

Autumn is the season of harvest. The intensity of Summer is past. We are preparing for Winter. There are tasks to be completed. We are readying ourselves for hibernation.

The small circle to the upper right of the large Yin/Yang tells us what we need in this time of transition. For balance in Summer, the season of maximum Yang, we need a diet with a preponderance of Yin energy. Now in Autumn, we are heading towards Winter when the opposite power will prevail and Yin energy will change our lives. To maintain balance, our diet will shift to one in which Yang foods predominate. The Autumn months should be the time in which we carefully prepare ourselves for this transformation. Thus the little circle that represents the nature of our seasonal diet shows light equally balanced with dark.

Our bodies start to slow down in Autumn. We are tired from the excesses of Summer. Now we need energy to prepare ourselves for the cold and penetrating damp of Winter. We will need to be protected not only on the outside, but inside as well. If we have been ill or are weak after Summer, we need to take special care to replenish our energy in Autumn. The body needs time for this adaptation and the long spell after Summer enables us to draw inward and prepare.

Autumn is still a time for liquids. They are the natural cleansers of the body. It is a time to be comforted. We appreciate warm vegetables in these months and the Chinese speciality Jown – little parcels of rice wrapped in bamboo leaves. Autumn cooking uses spice, but adds a little sweetness which we need to increase our supply of energy and bring harmony to this time of change.

The recipes in this section have been selected as sample seasonal dishes that will help your body leave Summer behind and prepare itself for the needs of Winter.

ALL RECIPES SERVE 4 PEOPLE

FRENCH TOAST

This is a universally popular dish, sustaining and satisfying for breakfast, equally good for lunch or a late night snack. Use the bread your family prefers, white or brown, but avoid using bread with a hard crust as it makes for difficulty in eating. Don't think that you can solve this by trimming off the crust; if you do, the slices of bread will disintegrate.

4 eggs
4 thick slices of bread
peanut or vegetable oil for frying
butter and honey to serve

Heat the wok, add 2 tablespoons oil, and swirl it around to coat the surface. Turn the heat down to medium. Break each egg into a small bowl to check if it is good. Then put them all into one bowl and beat until the whites and yolks are combined.

Dip each slice of bread into the beaten egg, turning it over carefully to allow the egg to soak in, then transfer to a plate.

Fry one side of the bread until it is golden brown, then fry the other side. Lift the fried bread from the wok with a slotted spoon, letting the excess oil drip away. Spread with butter and honey and serve at once.

Use unsalted butter and unblended honey for good flavor, or forget the butter and just spread with honey or condensed milk. Or just sprinkle with turbinado sugar for a crunchy texture.

JOWN

If you have ever looked into a freezer in a Chinese supermarket and wondered what the dark green leaf pyramids tied with string are – here is the answer. Jown are little packages of meat, rice and mung beans, expertly wrapped in bamboo leaves. They make a wonderful breakfast, and keep you feeling full and warm for hours.

In China there is a legend about jown – there was once a noble subject, an advisor to the king. The king ignored his good advice and listened to bad advisors. The "noble patriot" was so distressed that on 5 May he lost the will to live and jumped into the river. Jown are made on 5 May (in the Chinese calendar) and thrown into the water. They are eaten by the fish who are then too full to eat the body of the noble patriot. The dragon boats honor this same noble patriot, their many oars moving through the water frighten the fish away.

Jown are still eaten in May, although the weather is warm. To celebrate the festival, women of the extended families gather together and make up large batches.

The ingredients for jown are readily available in Chinese supermarkets. It is probably not worth attempting this recipe unless you are fairly "good with your hands." However, if your bundles are not neatly pyramidal they will still taste wonderful. People who are very skilled at making jown use just one large bamboo leaf, here we suggest using two. It is a good idea to buy a ready made jown and study its construction before trying it yourself.

When the jown are cooked, allow them to stand in the water while it cools. Remove the parcels, cut the string and carefully remove the bamboo leaves before serving. You can keep the bamboo-wrapped, cooked jown in the refrigerator for several days to allow the flavor to develop. To reheat them, simmer for 20–30 minutes.

To make 10 jown you will need:
20 bamboo leaves

2 lb. sticky (glutinous) rice
1 cup split mung beans
¾ lb. pork belly – about 2 slices
10 dried Chinese mushrooms
10 dried chestnuts

marinade for the pork:
2 tablespoons dark soy sauce
1 teaspoon cornstarch mixed with
1 tablespoon water
1 teaspoon five spice powder
½ teaspoon turbinado or light brown sugar
1 teaspoon salt
string for tying the parcels

Soak the mushrooms and chestnuts in water for 1½–2 hours. Wash the rice and the mung beans and put them to soak in separate bowls for half an hour.

About 20 minutes before you are you going to make the jown, cut the pork into pieces, about 1 inch × 2 inches. Put these into a bowl with the marinade ingredients and stir well to coat all the pieces.

To assemble the jown, the bamboo leaves need to be pliable. Boil some water in a wok or a wide pot, add the bamboo leaves, turn off the heat and leave for 5 minutes; this will both soften and sterilize them. Now drain the rice, mung beans, chestnuts, mushrooms, and bamboo leaves.

Take two bamboo leaves and lay them end to end overlapping each other by about 4 in. Bend the long ends of the leaves around to make a deep scoop.

Holding the scoop in one hand, spread a thin round layer of sticky rice, next a layer of mung beans. Now place a piece of meat, a mushroom and a chestnut at the center of the beans. Add another layer of beans, then rice. It is important to have a complete outer layer of rice to seal in the meat juices and absorb the flavor of the bamboo leaves.

Now carefully fold the long ends of the leaves over each other, and tuck them in. Tie the bundle tightly with string. Until you are experienced it may be best to ask someone to do this while you hold the bundle.

Put plenty of water in a large pot and bring to a boil, add four of the jown and simmer for 4 hours. Check the pot and add more water as necessary

VARIATION

Try filling the bundles with Chinese dried sausage, pork belly and chicken wings. These make a delicious combination.

FISH SOUP WITH CILANTRO

This is a delicately flavored soup, best made with a firm, textured fish such as cod, haddock, halibut, or sea bass. Freshwater fish like carp is another favorite. In this recipe the fish is marinated before cooking to enhance the flavor of the stock and to tenderize and improve the texture of the fish. The soup is very quick to make. Take care not to overcook the fish or it will tend to be tough. This soup is very nutritious and healthy.

½ lb. skinned fish fillet

for the marinade:
¼ teaspoon salt
¼ teaspoon sugar
a few drops soy sauce
I teaspoon cornstarch dissolved in
I tablespoon water

a few sprigs fresh cilantro
5 cups water

Slice the fish thinly. It is easier to do this if it is partially frozen (put into freezer for half an hour). If using frozen fish, slice while the fish is still a little frozen. The slices should be no bigger than 2 in. square.

In a shallow bowl, mix together the ingredients for the marinade, add the fish and stir gently to coat the pieces. Cover the dish and and put it into the refrigerator for half an hour.

Wash the cilantro and, if the stems are very long, shorten them by cutting in half.

Pour the water into a pot and bring to a boil. Add the marinated fish slices and bring back to a boil. Now add the sprigs of cilantro, turn down the heat and simmer gently for 2–3 minutes until the fish becomes opaque and is cooked.

Transfer the soup to a heated bowl and serve.

Top left, Eggplant with black bean sauce; top right, Potato pork; bottom right, Fish soup with cilantro; bottom left, Ham and tofu with mushroom sauce; center, Peanut pudding.

POTATO PORK

This is a substantial and comforting dish.

½ lb. pork belly, or shoulder if you
prefer a leaner cut

for the marinade:
I tablespoon dark soy sauce
I teaspoon salt
I teaspoon sugar
I teaspoon cornstarch dissolved in
I tablespoon cold water

4 small- to medium-sized (I lb.) potatoes
2 medium-sized onions
2 tablespoons oil
⅔ cup water
I teaspoon light soy sauce
I teaspoon sugar
2 scallions

VARIATION

*In this version the meat is briefly cooked
first, to make the flavors more distinct. You can
use beef but not chicken, as it is too bland.*

½ lb. sliced beef, marinated

*Heat the wok and add 1 tablespoon oil,
stir-fry the beef for 2 minutes, remove and drain.
Clean the wok, reheat it and add
2 tablespoons oil. Over a high heat stir-fry
the potatoes until they are golden all over.
Add 1 cup of water, 1 teaspoon light soy
sauce, 1 teaspoon sugar, cover and cook until
the potatoes are tender (about 20 minutes). Add
the onion and the beef, stir, cover,
and cook for 5 minutes.*

Cut the pork into ½ in. cubes, put them into
a bowl, add the marinade ingredients and
stir well.

Peel the potatoes and cut them into ¾ in.
chunks, put them into a colander and pour
boiling water over them to prevent them
discoloring.

Cut the onions in half through the root, trim
off the root and peel off the skin. Cut each
half into three lengthwise and cut each piece
in half.

Heat the wok, add 2 tablespoons oil, and swirl
it around to coat the whole surface. Over
high heat, fry the potatoes until they are
golden brown all over. Remove the potatoes
to a plate.

Stir-fry the pork briefly, now add ⅔ cup
water, 1 teaspoon light soy sauce and 1
teaspoon sugar. Turn the heat to low, cover,
and cook for 12 minutes.

Uncover the wok and add the potatoes, stir,
and cook for a further 8 minutes. Now add
the onions, cover, and cook for 5 minutes.

Lastly, wash and chop the green parts of the
scallions into 1 in. lengths, add them to the
wok, stir briefly, transfer to a heated plate,
and serve.

The character of this dish will vary
considerably depending on whether the
potatoes are waxy or floury in texture. Floury
potatoes will give it a nice, soupy quality.

EGGPLANT WITH BLACK BEAN SAUCE

This recipe is best using Chinese eggplants which are smaller and sweeter than the readily available, plump purple ones.

They are fairly long and much narrower (see p. 105) and can vary in color from purple to white. As they have fewer seeds and a sweeter flavor there is no need to salt and rinse them, unlike their purple relatives whose flesh tends to be bitter.

This is a very rich-tasting and delicious way to cook eggplants.

½ tablespoon fermented black
beans (around 25–30 beans)
4 cloves garlic
I medium onion
I scallion
5 tablespoons oil
I small- to medium-sized eggplant
2 tablespoons water
I teaspoon salt
I teaspoon sugar
I teaspoon light soy sauce

Rinse the beans and dry them. Using the flat side of a heavy knife or cleaver, tap each clove of garlic and remove the skin. Put the beans with the garlic into a small bowl and, using the wooden handle of the knife or cleaver, mash them together and set aside.

Cut through the root of the onion to halve it and peel back the skin. Trim off the root and top. Cut each half crosswise into three and each part into six pieces.

Wash the scallion and trim off the root, chop it roughly.

Heat the wok and add 5 tablespoons of oil. Quickly roll cut (see p. 79) the eggplant into 2 in. wedges.

Add the beans and garlic to the wok, stir-fry for 10 seconds. Now add the onion and eggplant. Stir for a moment and add 2 tablespoons water, stir well, and leave to cook for 3 minutes.

Add the scallion, the salt, sugar, and light soy sauce, gently stir them in. Transfer to a heated dish and serve.

HAM AND TOFU WITH MUSHROOM SAUCE

This light and nutritious dish is quick and easy to prepare.

2 dried Chinese mushrooms
¼ lb. slice of Canadian bacon or ham
4 oz. block tofu
I scallion
3 teaspoons oil
I teaspoon salt
I teaspoon sugar
I teaspoon light soy sauce or oyster sauce
I teaspoon cornstarch mixed with
I tablespoon water
a little sesame oil

Clean the mushrooms and leave them to soak in a cup of cold water for at least an hour or overnight. When they have softened lift them out, remove the woody stalks and discard them. Slice the tops thinly. Strain the mushroom water to remove any grit and return the sliced mushrooms to it. You will be using the soaking water to make the sauce.

Slice the ham into ⅛ in. slices measuring about 1½ in. square. Slice the tofu into ⅜ in. slices. Arrange the tofu and ham alternately on an oval plate, overlapping the slices in two adjacent rows. Drizzle 1 teaspoon of oil over the top.

Prepare the steamer and bring it to a boil. Put the plate of ham and tofu in to steam (see page 86) for 7 minutes.

Wash the scallion, trim off the root and chop it finely.

Heat the wok, add 2 teaspoons oil. Add the sliced mushrooms and their water and bring to a boil. Now add 1 teaspoon each of salt, sugar and light soy or oyster sauce, bring back to a boil and add the chopped scallion.

Pour the cornstarch mixture into the wok and stir to thicken the sauce.

Remove the plate of ham and tofu from the steamer and pour the sauce over it. Carefully put the hot plate onto a slightly larger one and serve. If you like, you can sprinkle with a little sesame oil.

PEANUT PUDDING

This syrupy, nutty custard-style pudding is quick and nutritious. It uses peanut butter and rock sugar. Choose a peanut butter that does not have artificial additives for the best flavor, smooth or crunchy, depending on whether you like a smooth or slightly nutty texture.

If you are allergic to peanuts, you can make this pudding in exactly the same way using light tahini (sesame seed paste), which produces a delicious flavor. Otherwise, try making it with ground almonds or cashew nuts for a mild-tasting pudding, or ground walnuts or hazelnuts for something stronger. Ground almonds give an especially delicious result.

This pudding uses rock sugar, available in Chinese supermarkets (see p. 92), and this gives the authentic flavor. But you could use natural turbinado or light brown sugar instead. You can vary the amount of sugar to taste.

4 cups water
4 oz. rock sugar
I cup peanut butter, smooth or crunchy
a little cornstarch mixed in cold water to thicken
(if you like a thicker pudding)

Pour the water into a pot and bring it to a boil. Add the rock sugar and simmer until all the sugar has melted.

Now add the peanut butter and and bring to a boil; the peanut butter should dissolve into the syrup.

Mix a little cornstarch with cold water and stir it into the liquid slowly to get the thickness you prefer.

VARIATION I

using tahini

Simply replace the peanut butter with light tahini, thinning the tahini if necessary by stirring in a little of the sugar syrup.

VARIATION 2

using ground almonds, cashews, walnuts or hazelnuts

Replace the peanut butter with 2½ cups of ground almonds, cashews, walnuts or hazelnuts. Pour the syrup onto the ground nuts, mixing well. Return to the pot, add the cornstarch mixture, stirring well over a gentle heat until thickened.

In Winter our bodies close up. We are more tense. Our blood flows more slowly in our arteries and veins. We need greater supplies of energy to keep us warm and protect us from the cold. Not surprisingly these are the months when we use up far more energy and need to restock our fuel. We have a hunger for Yang foods that have a higher quantity of fats and grease. We like deep fried dishes and ones that are strongly flavored and sweet.

Winter is the season for hot drinks. We can feel the boost they give to our circulation almost after the first sip. Our natural intelligence tells us to avoid iced drinks. They slow our digestion and make our blood sluggish. Warm foods, like warm drinks, also have a beneficial effect on our circulation and thus ease the pressure on our hearts. In the midst of Winter, we find ourselves warmed and relaxed.

The recipes in this section have been selected as sample seasonal dishes that will relax you and give your body the energy and protection it needs throughout the Winter months.

When Yang has been completely transformed into Yin, there is a season of fullness. This is Winter. "In Winter," says the physician of the Yellow Emperor, "the pulse of the stomach should be small like a stone. Then it will be healthy and well-balanced." He warns: "The illnesses of Winter recur in the Springtime."

Winter is the season of regeneration. The natural world withdraws into itself. It is the season of inner growth.

Our bodies are different in Winter. We protect ourselves against the influences of the weather, the cold winds, the seeping mist, the hard frost. It is a time of survival.

The small circle to the lower right of the large Yin/Yang tells us what we need in Winter. We have come through the transitional months of Autumn when our diet was an equal balance of Yin and Yang to help us manage the shift from Summer to Winter. Now in the Winter months, Yin energy is at its fullest. Our diet changes to one in which Yang foods predominate. Thus the little circle shows a preponderance of light and a smaller proportion of dark.

ALL RECIPES SERVE 4 PEOPLE

SALTY PORRIDGE

Porridge is a wonderfully warming dish for those really cold wintry days. It is quick and easy to prepare, making it a perfect dish to cook at breakfast time. It keeps up your energy levels during the morning, and here, with the added extra of protein in the form of a little pork or chicken, it makes a complete meal.

Choose quick-cooking oatmeal for convenience. However, you could use coarser oats or jumbo oats, and the cooking could then be speeded up simply by soaking the oats overnight in the water before cooking. If using prepacked porridge oats, check the instructions on the packet for cooking times.

2 oz. lean chicken or pork
4 cups water
I teaspoon salt
I heaped cup oatmeal

Mince chop the meat with a cleaver.

Bring the water and the salt to a boil in a large pot. Add the meat and cook for a few minutes until it changes color.

Sprinkle the oatmeal into the water, stirring well, and bring back to a boil. Cover the pot, remove from the heat, and allow the porridge to stand for 5 minutes.

Do not stir once you have taken the pot off the heat.

Taste and add more salt if you like, then serve.

RICE NOODLES, SINGAPORE STYLE

Colorful and tasty, this dish is quick to prepare once you have assembled all the ingredients. You may be able to buy char siu (Chinese barbecued pork) in Chinese markets or specialty stores. However, you can substitute a well-flavored ham or barbecued pork for the char siu.

½ lb. shrimp, fresh or frozen
8 oz. rice noodles
2 eggs
¼ lb. char siu
I medium-sized onion
2 scallions
2 tablespoons oil
2 teaspoons light soy sauce
I ½ teaspoons salt
I tablespoon curry sauce
a few sesame seeds

If you are using frozen shrimp, you can spread them on a plate and leave at room temperature for 30 minutes. Or, to speed things along, put them into a strainer and plunge them into a pot of cold water. Leave them for a few minutes, drain and spread them out on a plate.

In a large pot, boil plenty of water, add the rice noodles and stir to separate them.

Take the pot off the heat and allow the noodles to stand in the water for 3 minutes. Lift a noodle and test to see if it is cooked. When the noodles are ready, tip them into a colander to drain, quickly rinse in cold water and set them aside to drain.

Peel and slice the onion thinly. Wash the scallions and cut off the roots. Cut the scallions into 1½ in. lengths. Slice the char sui into long thin strips. Beat the eggs.

Heat the wok, add 1 tablespoon oil, add the beaten eggs and cook gently over a low heat without stirring. Remove the omelette from the wok with a slotted spoon, allow it to cool, then slice thinly.

Heat the wok, add 1 tablespoon oil, and swirl it around to cover the whole surface. Put the onions, scallions and drained noodles into the wok and stir-fry for 2–3 minutes. Add 2 teaspoons light soy sauce, 1½ teaspoons salt, 1 tablespoon curry sauce, and stir-fry.

Finally add the char siu, sliced omelette and shrimp. Stir-fry to heat them all through.

Remove to a heated plate, sprinkle with the sesame seeds and serve.

HOT AND SOUR SOUP

This soup can be as hot as you like, just increase the amount of chili to suit your taste. It is wonderful for clearing bronchial passages and stuffed noses. Most of the ingredients are ones which you can keep in your cupboard or freezer.

Red rice vinegar, wood ears and canned bamboo shoots are available in Chinese grocery stores. You may have difficulty in buying char siu, unless you have access to specialty Chinese food stores. However, you can substitute a good quality ham or barbecued pork.

Once you have all the ingredients ready the soup should take only 4 minutes to cook.

1 small wood ear (see p. 93)
¼ cup frozen peas
½ cup frozen shrimp
½ cup bamboo shoots (canned)
a 1 in. cube of tofu
¼ lb. char siu (Chinese barbecued pork)
2 small eggs
1 small fresh red chili
1 tablespoon dark soy sauce
2½ cups water
1 teaspoon cornstarch mixed with
1 tablespoon water
2 tablespoons red rice vinegar
ground white pepper to taste

Choose one small wood ear and put it to soak in a bowl of cold water. It will need at least 30 minutes to reconstitute or you can soak it overnight. Squeeze the excess water from the mushroom and cut it into small pieces.

Defrost the frozen peas and shrimp. If you are short of time, measure them into a colander, pour cold water over them, and leave to drain.

Drain the bamboo shoots, rinse, and slice thinly.

Cut a 1 in. square piece of tofu from the block and slice it thinly. You can store the remaining tofu in a bowl of fresh water in the refrigerator for 2–3 days.

Thinly slice the char siu.

Break the eggs into a bowl and beat them to combine yolk and white.

Wash the chili, cut off the stem, and slice the pepper finely across the pod. Wash the board, knife, and your hands before doing anything else. Bring 2½ cups water to a boil in a pot. Add the pork, shrimp, bamboo shoots, tofu, peas, wood ear, soy sauce, and chili. Cook for 2 minutes over medium heat.

Now slowly pour in the beaten egg in a thin stream, stirring continuously with a chopstick or fork. The egg will cook into flaky strands.

Add the dissolved cornstarch and stir to thicken the soup slightly.

Turn off the heat and add the vinegar, stirring briefly. Transfer to a heated bowl and serve.

PEACE AND WELL-BEING FOR YOUNG AND OLD

This delicate and juicy dish is very quick and simple to prepare, nourishing and easy to digest. It uses cilantro, which in Chinese cuisine is the classic accompaniment to fish and seafood. When cooked, the cilantro loses its rather pungent smell. It is important to check that the plate you plan to use will fit inside your steamer (see p. 86 for advice on steaming).

1 lb. skinned fillet of cod
½ pack of tofu (about 5 oz.)
a few sprigs of cilantro, washed
1 scallion
2 teaspoons oil
a little light soy sauce
½ teaspoon salt
pepper

VARIATION

You can make this dish as a fishcake. Steam the fish with just the cilantro and chopped scallion. Remove the plate from the steamer and mash the steamed fish with the tofu, a little salt, pepper, and oil. Add a little beaten egg so that the mixture will stick together. Press the mixture into a small shallow dish and steam for 5 minutes.

On the other hand, you may be able to buy fish "paste" in a Chinese supermarket. Just mix the paste with the other ingredients and steam for 5 minutes.

Rinse the fish and pat it dry with paper towels.

Drain the tofu and cut it in half horizontally, then cut one of the halves into slices about ½ in. thick by 3 in. long. Put the remaining half into a bowl of fresh water, cover, and store in the refrigerator, it will keep for 2–3 days.

Wash the cilantro and chop them coarsely.

Wash the scallion and trim off the root. Slice both the green and white parts thinly

Lay the slices of tofu on a small plate, side by side to form a base for the fish. Lay the fish on top of the tofu. Sprinkle a little oil, then the cilantro and chopped scallion on the fish.

Set up your steamer (see p. 86). When the water is boiling, place the plate of fish into the steamer and cook for 5 minutes, or until the fish is done.

Remove the steamer from the heat and carefully remove the plate, which will be very hot! Lay the plate on a slightly larger plate to serve.

Sprinkle a little soy sauce, salt and pepper over the fish, and serve immediately.

STEWED BEAN CURD WITH LAMB

Traditionally, a belly cut of lamb, trimmed of its fat, would be used for this dish. As this is not easily available everywhere you can use shoulder or leg as a substitute. It is up to you whether to include the bone. If you do, use a cleaver or heavy sharp knife to chop the meat with bone into small pieces.

This protein-rich dish is very good for sustaining your energy during Winter and settling and soothing the stomach. It features two bean curd products, dried bean curd sticks, and fermented bean curd (see p. 98).

around 14 8 in.-long pieces (4 oz.) dried
bean curd sticks
1½–2 lb. boned shoulder or sirloin or
butt end of leg of lamb
6 in. piece fresh ginger root
3 pints water
2 tablespoons oil
3 cubes of fermented bean curd
1 scallion, cut into shortish (1 in.) lengths
a little light soy sauce

VARIATION

Sometimes you can buy bean curd sticks which have been deep-fried. These keep their shape better during the long cooking of this dish. You can deep-fry the sticks yourself. As soon as they are puffed up, remove and drain them. To remove excess oil, wait for the sticks to cool, put them in a pot of cold water and squeeze vigorously – the oil will come out and float on the surface of the water. Repeat this process until you have removed most of the oil, then cut the sticks into 2 in. lengths and proceed with the recipe.

Rinse the bean curd sticks and soak them in a roasting pot filled with cold water until they are soft (about 5 minutes). Then lift them out and, using scissors, cut them into 2 in. lengths.

Cut the lamb into 1 in. cubes, or ask your butcher to do this.

Slice the ginger across the grain into ⅛ in. slices. There is no need to peel it.

Boil 5 cups of water in a large pot. Add the lamb and boil for 2 minutes. Drain in a metal colander, then rinse the meat with cold water. Set aside to drain.

Heat the wok and add 2 tablespoons oil, swirling it around to coat the whole surface. Add the ginger slices and stir-fry for 1 minute. Now add the cubes of fermented bean curd and mash them into the oil. Add the lamb and about 2½ cups of water. Bring to a boil over a high heat. Now lower the heat to a slow simmer, cover and leave to cook for 1½ hours or until the meat is tender.

Uncover the wok from time to time and, if the mixture is too dry, add a little water.

Lastly, add the pieces of scallion and stir. Transfer to a heated plate, sprinkle with a little light soy sauce and serve immediately.

Clockwise from top left: Stir-fried greens with garlic; Egg pudding with ginger; Rice noodles, Singapore style; Hot and sour soup; Stewed bean curd with lamb.

STIR-FRIED GREENS WITH GARLIC

The greens in this recipe are bok choy (see p. 101), they have crisp and juicy white stems, and rich-tasting dark green leaves. If you can't find bok choy you can use Swiss chard, although the stems are thinner and stringier, and will not be so beautifully crisp. If the bok choy are very small you can cook the leaves whole, although this makes them much trickier to eat with chopsticks!

1 in. piece fresh ginger root
6–8 cloves of garlic (to taste)
1 lb. bok choy
2 tablespoons oil
½ teaspoon salt
1 teaspoon sugar

Clean the piece of ginger root and cut it across the grain into 4–5 slices. There is no need to peel it.

Using the flat side of a heavy knife or cleaver, tap each clove of garlic and remove the skin.

Trim the root from the bok choy and snap off the leafy stems; wash them carefully and shake off the water. If the leaves are big, with long stems, cut the stems from the leaves and, if the stems are very long, cut them into 2 in. pieces.

Heat the wok, add 2 tablespoons oil, and swirl it around so that all the surface is oiled.

Lower the heat to medium, add the slices of ginger, and stir-fry until the ginger releases its fragrance.

Now add the garlic cloves and stir-fry for 1 minute.

Add the white stems of the bok choy and stir-fry for 1 minute. Put on the lid and cook for a further minute.

Next add the leaves, salt and sugar and stir-fry for 1 minute, or until the leaves are wilted.

Quickly stir, transfer to a heated plate and serve.

EGG PUDDING WITH GINGER

This is a very light, refreshing custard, steamed rather than baked in the more usual style. It uses a ginger syrup for its base, which is made from ginger root sweetened with rock sugar, which you will need to look for in a Chinese supermarket.

If you can't find rock sugar, you could use natural turbinado sugar instead, although the taste will be significantly different. If you enjoy this dish, you may want to experiment with different sugars – but we are sure you will find that rock sugar gives the best flavor.

2 cups water
an 8 in. piece (4 oz.) fresh ginger root
4 oz. rock sugar
4 large eggs
⅔ cup milk
a few drops vegetable oil

Clean the ginger and slice it into ⅛ in.-thick slices across the grain. There is no need to peel it.

If the rock sugar is in very large lumps, you may cover it with a clean cloth and smash it with a rolling pin so that it will dissolve more quickly.

Pour the water into a pot and bring it to a boil. Add the ginger slices and boil for 2 minutes. With a slotted spoon, remove the ginger slices and discard them.

Add the rock sugar to the boiling water and, when it has all melted, remove the pot from the heat.

Set up your steamer (see p. 86), add water, and bring it to a boil.

Break the eggs separately to check that they are good, then put them into one bowl and whisk.

Add the milk to the pot of ginger syrup and slowly pour in the eggs, whisking all the while. Continue to whisk and add a few drops of oil.

Carefully pour the mixture into 4 small bowls and place them in the top of the steamer. Cook for 4 minutes. Be careful when lifting out the bowls, they will be very hot. You can serve this pudding hot or cold.

AUTHORS' ACKNOWLEDGMENTS

We are often asked if Feng Shui will survive its transplant from the East to the West. Even in China, history has been harsh on Feng Shui. Many of its masters now live abroad.

Feng Shui grows out of a rich, complex culture. It cannot be surgically removed from the body of that culture because it is intimately connected with other arts such as astrology, numerology, and traditional Chinese medicine. The understanding of energy, which forms the basis of Feng Shui, provides the deep, unseen root of all these arts. Without an underlying appreciation of this foundation, it is not really possible to practice authentic Feng Shui.

Then there is the question of training. The four masters whose wisdom has influenced our book have made Feng Shui their life's work. Typically, the training takes about 30 years. You learn through close association with your masters, in a way that is similar to the apprenticeship system. You simply cannot get anywhere beyond the most elementary ideas from a weekend workshop, a row of books, or even a few years' research. Many people in the West fail to understand this, perhaps because they think that the goal of learning is data collection rather than wisdom.

It is because of these concerns that we have tried, with the help of Gaia Books, to present the fundamental principles of Feng Shui in three books: *The Feng Shui Handbook*, *The Personal Feng Shui Manual*, and *The Feng Shui Kitchen*. Our aim is to show very simply how the profound wisdom of Feng Shui can be adapted to life in contemporary society.

For this opportunity, we are immeasurably grateful to Joss Pearson, Managing Director, Pip Morgan, Managing Editor, and Patrick Nugent, Art Director.

Much of the collaborative effort that has gone into these books has taken place around a table at The Immortals restaurant in London's Chinatown and we call ourselves "the Immortals team." In addition to our family of three sons – Lam Tin Yun, Lam Tin Yu, and Lam Tin Hun – we have two other team members. Bridget Morley has designed all three books with great patience and sensitivity. For *The Feng Shui Kitchen*, she also took on the task of working with us to discuss, draft, and test all the recipes as well as the section on selecting and preparing ingredients. Her understanding and skill have made this book possible. The other member of our team is Richard Reoch, who has been willing to devote himself wholeheartedly to our efforts at cross-cultural communication. He has spent countless hours translating the concepts and practices of our tradition into a universal idiom that clearly has been understood and appreciated in the many countries where these books have now been published.

Finally, we wish to pay tribute to the many teachers in China, Hong Kong, and Taiwan from whom we have learned and to whose profound knowledge we have done our best to be faithful in our work.

ABOUT THE AUTHORS

Lam Kam Chuen and Lam Kai Sin were both born in Hong Kong after the Second World War. They first met as young teenagers while studying martial arts and married in the early 1970s. Together, they have studied an extraordinary range of classical Chinese arts, ranging from Tai Chi and Chi Kung to traditional Chinese medicine and Feng Shui. They run The Immortals restaurant, a recently restored venue on the site of one of the very first Chinese restaurants established in London's West End theater district.

FENG SHUI CONSULTATIONS AND ADVICE

Anyone wanting an individual consultation with Master Lam for their home or business may contact him at: The Immortals, 58–60 Shaftesbury Avenue, London W1V 7DE, United Kingdom. Telephone: (44) 0831 802 598. Fax: (44) 0207 734 9578. He is often invited to travel in Europe and the United States for consultations and lectures. For details and fees, please send a self-addressed envelope to Master Lam.

PUBLISHER'S ACKNOWLEDGMENTS

The publishers would like to thank the authors and their son Tin Yu for their unfailing help and hospitality. Thanks go to the following people for their assistance in creating this book: Sara Matthews, Christine Smith, Delora Jones, and also all the staff at The Immortals restaurant.

PHOTO CREDITS HONG KONG TOURIST ASSOCIATION: pp. 8, 67. IMAGE BANK: CTP, pp. 7, 110–11, 88 (bottom), 115; B. Froomer, p. 88 (top); Guang Hui Xie, pp. 6, 12–13, 34–5, 147; Guido Rossi, p. 137; Mahaux Photo, p. 127; Yuan Hao Ma, p. 6 (left), 72–3; Richard Reoch, p. 157. TELEGRAPH COLOUR LIBRARY: Silvain Grandadan, p. 67; Keith Macgregor, p. 89; VCL, p. 88 (middle). TONY STONE IMAGES: John Lamb, p. 47 (left); Joel Larson, p. 66; Yann Layma, p. 2; Ed Pritchard, pp. 46–7. ELIZABETH WHITING: p. 47 (right).

ILLUSTRATIONS Images on pp. 22 and 31, courtesy of Master Lam. Watercolour sketches by Bridget Morley.

INDEX